Everyday Enchantments

T0127499

What people are saying about

Everyday Enchantments

Maria DeBlassie has crafted magic within the pages of her new book, *Everyday Enchantments*. Her eloquent words offer the "promise of soul replenishment" as one traverses the journey of her – and their – metaphorical metamorphosis. Page after page, readers will experience the soothing balm of DeBlassie's words as they encourage one to open her heart, her mind, her ear, her thoughts and her soul to the unique transpersonal book they hold in their hands. Just as DeBlassie mentions early on in *Everyday Enchantments* when writing of the unexpected delight of discovering a double yolk, her heartfelt writing is like "cradling ... gold" in one's hands.

Reading and absorbing the beauty of Maria DeBlassie's *Everyday Enchantments* will have readers conjuring their own magical life. Her words will caress their soul and embrace their heart with inspiration and encouragement. *Everyday Enchantments* blends together poetic consciousness such as from Maya Angelou and Mary Oliver all while weaving in powerful and deep inner wisdom such as from Clarissa Pinkola Estes. Yet, Maria DeBlassie beautifully stands out given the uniqueness of *Everyday Enchantments*. It's a must-read and a must to be gently and lovingly held in a sacred place of honor in one's personal library. DeBlassie's *Everyday Enchantments* is like a heart song that every woman should feel.
Janelle Alex, Ph.D. – The Writer's Shaman

An insightful collection of short writings that make you look at the everyday in a whole new light. Ponder how different life could be if you stop taking everything for granted and find joy in the simplicity of it all.
Erin Elliott, author of *The Sword of Lumina* series

Reading this enchanted collection is so much more than reading a book ... it's an unearthing of things half-remembered and bringing them into the light. Gorgeous and luminous ... thank you, Maria, for unwinding this spell for your readers.
Laura Bickle, critically-acclaimed author of *Nine of Stars*

To build everyday bridges between the magick and the mundane out of the long-sought and hard-won materials of will and wonder is the act of a true Priestess. In this book, DeBlassie offers rich glimpses of daily rituals, miniature spells in their own right that prompt the reader to look for the quiet divinity in their own lives, to see the subtle majesty in their day-to-day routines, and to question their perceived barriers between the modern and the mystical.
Danielle Dulsky, author of *Woman Most Wild*

Everyday Enchantments

Maria DeBlassie

MOON
BOOKS

Winchester, UK
Washington, USA

First published by Moon Books, 2018
Moon Books is an imprint of John Hunt Publishing Ltd., No. 3 East Street, Alresford
Hampshire SO24 9EE, UK
office1@jhpbooks.net
www.johnhuntpublishing.com
www.moon-books.net

For distributor details and how to order please visit the 'Ordering' section on our website.

Text copyright: Maria DeBlassie 2017

ISBN: 978 1 78535 923 1
978 1 78535 924 8 (ebook)
Library of Congress Control Number: 2017963043

All rights reserved. Except for brief quotations in critical articles or reviews, no part of this
book may be reproduced in any manner without prior written permission from the publishers.

The rights of Maria DeBlassie as author have been asserted in accordance with the Copyright,
Designs and Patents Act 1988.

A CIP catalogue record for this book is available from the British Library.

Design: Stuart Davies

Printed and bound by CPI Group (UK) Ltd, Croydon, CR0 4YY, UK

We operate a distinctive and ethical publishing philosophy in
all areas of our business, from our global network of authors to
production and worldwide distribution.

Contents

To the wild ones who make my everyday more magical.
You know who you are.

Everyday Enchantment

ENCHANTMENT: *A spell wrapped in a noun. Three syllables. One state of being.*

To live with Enchantment is to see beyond the bricks and mortar that make up your home and into the magic infused within its frame. It is made up of stories and dried bay leaves and dreams whispered into the heads of dandelions. Of bare feet on carpeted floors and the smell of burning sage. Crystals – amethyst, citrine, amazonite, smoky quartz – winding in and around your books; all the better to magnify their magic. It is to peel back the layers of your day-to-day and search for that elusive energy that winds its way up your spine and outward into your life. Let the snake at your base wriggle free of its coil to climb up to your shoulder blades and across your open back. There is no room for tightly stacked discs here, just the taste of joy when the sun licks your skin.

You might find it at the bottom of an empty teacup. Your future written in soggy leaves or in the whisper of trees, their leaves rustling and murmuring secrets only they can understand. Sometimes they are kind enough to translate for you – if you listen long enough. If you shower their roots with distilled love songs and feed them the black earth from your compost. It's there, too, when you run your tongue along the grooves and ridges of a well-loved sentence. It's everywhere. Even in the spaces you think have lost hope, like the junk drawer where you keep your faded dreams, stray screws, and half-forgotten heart-breaks along with wine corks and a few rubber bands. They're not lost, just resting like seeds in the earth before they are ready to break open.

That is the first syllable.

The second is to learn from Enchantment, to listen to Coyote's call when he plays his tricks. Coyote loves his tricks. And you should too. What delicious messages wrapped in matted fur and a lolling tongue! All he wants is for you to take that leap of faith when only you can see the soft earth on the other side of the cliff. Don't you know that you have wings? They are just rusty from disuse. Just listen to Coyote's long-winded stories (he does so admire himself) and watch the flick of his tail. All he asks is for you to trust him, even if he can't be trusted; his lesson is real, hard as onyx in your palm, ephemeral as the desert rain that you feel in your bones when all you see is a cloudless sky. No weatherman can ever map the storms and sunshine working their way across your body.

Coyote has no room for logic, just the reason in his unreason. Just those perfect coincidences set in motion by the padding of his paws. *You are raw power*, he says, *a spark of the universe set in motion*. And you must trust this power that is you, that is the earth, that is the beating of your heart. A rhythmic tattoo forever pounding out your path, however many times you try to stray from it. All Enchantment asks is that you absorb the wisdom of the moon and the stars, and the prophesying of the seeds burrowed deep in the dirt. Coyote is there to make sure you listen, even when the rest of the world prefers your ears stopped with cotton and your heart beating as slow as melting snow in winter.

And the third syllable? To conjure. Here you weave your spell with vowels and consonants and beeswax candles. You seal them with pure starlight and a handful of chamomile. Then you burn away the dry brush and the brittle ideas that don't hold up against the moonlight. There is no room here for literal ... *things* or the people who think them. Not if you want to create. Not if you want to believe that the most important part of your everyday occurs in the moments others can too easily overlook. (Seldom can you find a person strong enough to brave the stillness or wade into the bottomless waters of imagination.) You make your life here, in the infinite potential of seconds and minutes and hours unfurling into vines and roots. Because when you are looking for everyday enchantment, it finds you. Always. And if you let it, it will settle inside your skin and feed your soul with dreams grown ripe under the sun's caress. It drops you deep down into the rich earth and forgotten caves buried between heartbeats – places that many are too afraid to venture inside. For how can you absorb the marvelous, if you do not recognize it reflected in yourself, feel it settle in your bones like so much calcium?

That's Enchantment.

A three-syllable spell wrapped in a noun, planted in the earth and nourished with moonlight. Let the roots stretch to the underworld and the leaves unfurl toward the heavens. Walk across the star-kissed bridge made of hollyhock seeds and strong will. There is your passage into the unseen universe.

On Double Yolks

The skillet is hot – hot as the bluegrass playing in the background, hot as the black lightning coffee in your cup. Today is a day for a bold breakfast. You shake off your usual weekday oatmeal in favor of eggs over easy, chorizo, and toast. A small-town desert diner breakfast made all the better coming from your kitchen. You could get drunk on the scent of burning cedar in the air, that fireplace smell more evidence than anything that summer has faded into fall, though the trees have not yet turned their green leaves to flames.

There is an air of abundance to your morning. A welcome feeling after the exhaustion that seems to have settled in your bones with the changing of the seasons and the week's intense demands on your time and energy. Sometimes you feel as if dusty souls want to suck away your light, or at the very least, pile their debris upon you, since to them you seem so weightless. They don't know the work it takes to keep the corners of your mind free from grime and your schedule clean of mindless busy.

But forget all that. Today is a day for a hearty breakfast and devotion to your craft. You will fill yourself up with words and coffee to assuage the thinness that has crept into your soul, as if you are an empty cupboard, save for a few crumbs. You crack an egg over the sizzling pan with these thoughts heavy in your head, despite your attempts to fill your mind with the sunshine that saturates your home.

And there it is: a fat, golden double yolk.

The orbs sit piled atop one another as if caught kissing. You marvel at how so much yolk could fit into such a little eggshell. The broken pieces in your hand hardly seem capable of cradling such gold. They appear too fragile and yet birthed more than others thought they could hold. You can't tell where one yolk ends and the other begins; you are mystified by this anomaly.

You watch your eggs cook, and a sly voice inside your head – the one who loves a good story, the one who can't resist the lure of superstition – coyly whispers that double yolks are good luck, harbingers of double the grace, the plenty, the fortune. These are the stories of old wives, crones, and witches that you are half-tempted to believe, if only because these fat yolks nestled together in front of you seem nothing short of magic themselves. Another part of you – the one descended from those old crones, healers, and potential witches – knows it would be foolish to ignore such a gift. And it is a gift. A reminder.

You flip your eggs and decide to let your fanciful imagination run away with you, feeling the tension loosen from your shoulders as you do so. Yes, you commit to the idea. Double yolks *are* good luck. All at once, you are grateful for this message. This little sign that you are not a bare cupboard after all, but a fully stocked larder – if it is ever appropriate to compare yourself to food storage. No matter.

You are abundance. You are luck. You are double the fortune. Hard week be damned.

On Synchronicity

It is the moment between thinking of moving in one direction – *perhaps I will rekindle that relationship after all* – and then being stopped by a red light at the crosswalk – *don't go down that road*. In truth, you know how it will end, although you can't help toying with the idea. It is the ladybug that lands on your porch as you turn your thoughts to a new piece of writing. *Yes*, it says. *Yes*.

You are grateful for that flash of insight helping you hone your creative path that has long since diverged from the mainstream. Grateful for your fluency in a language too few know how to speak. Your day is nothing without this never-ending conversation between yourself and the universe or the clap of thunder that punctuates your off-the-cuff revelations. You cannot speak your truth without lightning striking both in your blood and in your sky. It is terrifying consciousness. Pure insight. And sometimes it is just the song that blares from your car radio when you key the ignition – *there's no going back*, the lyrics roll out – just as you marvel at how your life is a series of forward moving steps, though it sometimes feels like more of a cha-cha.

The clock ticking in the middle of the night, its hands pushing you out of sleep with their hushed staccato, asks you what is worth your time, and sometimes, why you continue to waste it on unimportant things. You cannot hide in the darkness. It only serves to illuminate what matters. Like the clicking clock. A mechanical heartbeat sounding from a relic that you know doesn't work in the light of day. There are no plugs or batteries to operate it, and you have long since given up winding it. But in the moonlight it still ticks, as if charged by electric dreams.

It is everywhere and nowhere. A wisp of silk that guides you if you know how to unravel the spool. A collection of signs, like cards in a tarot deck, meant only for your eyes. Understood only by your gut. You allow this skill to blossom inside you, the ability to translate these letters from the universe that will only reach you if you leave your mailbox open. Ask your questions without censor or clear reason. Just be ready for answers.

Synchronicity is the roadrunner that greets you one morning as you head to your office. You pause to enjoy the beautiful morning, the way the mint green of the trees highlights the rich purple of the mountains, the turquoise sky a perfect backdrop. A thought flits through your brain – an old, worn thought that has outlived its welcome. It has muscled its way in nonetheless, no doubt from the backdoor you left open from overwork the day before. It is a thought from a past self, a small shadow of a doubt on an otherwise gorgeous day. A tiny little question mark that almost suffocates your latest pop of inspiration.

And then the roadrunner crosses your path. It darts past you from bush to rock to dry brush as you lock your car, confusing evil spirits by its X-shaped feet, leaving them unable to tell in which direction you are moving, casting away darkness and welcoming light. *All is well*, it says. *Follow the inspiration and all is well. No darkness can find you while you cultivate the light.* So you turn from that shadowy thought – it is irrelevant – and wrap your inspiration around you like a leather coat protecting you from the inconstant weather of your thoughts, too often tainted by what you absorb from others. These are not your feelings, you realize, not your burden, nor your path to untangle. You must go beyond the white noise and recognize yourself in the early morning hush and quick dance of this long-tailed bird. You thank the roadrunner for his visit. You thank the universe for sending this message. You thank yourself for listening.

Crocheting Infinite Blankets

Each stitch is a piece of woven intention. A slip of yarn looped around another to bind your thoughts into the blankets you create. Healing, nourishing, abundant thoughts. They are tapestries of a happy life you conjure every time you pick up your needle and yarn, a comforting hug you can wrap around yourself when the night is cold or the day long. They have no beginning or end. Just the soft ridges of braided cotton.

Your first was a monstrous purple affair, crocheted with only a series of what you now know are half-stitches. But you and your sisters were set on crocheting your own infinite blankets after watching the heroine in *Like Water for Chocolate* knit an endless blanket and ride off into the sunset with her creation blazing behind her. Yes, you needed blankets like that. You needed proof of your story. And so you rustled together old crochet hooks from your mother's abandoned stash and bought skeins of multicolored yarn and crocheted for years and years. But while the heroine of that story poured her grief into each loop and tied it off with despair, you created joy through each imperfect stitch. And you left plenty of room for your desires to bloom in between the loosely connected loops. It's never a good idea to hold on to anything too tightly, after all, nor map it too precisely.

Together, you crocheted hopes for love and adventure and deep living into the folds of your blankets. You used the yarn to cast out lines for the lives you yearned to grow into once you left home. With each stitch, you freed yourself from the burden of your ancestors' stories, and the narratives they felt you should live out – those hollow, empty things like graves or debilitating traditions. So much made with a self-taught half-stitch. Not even a real stitch at all, some said. That didn't stop you from making a whole story with it.

That was your blanket woven with sister love and the unburdened glee of youth. None of you even minded that your blankets were a mishmash of colors and textures as you learned how to loop a proper, even stitch. Tried, anyway. After two or three years of busily working on your infinite blanket, while watching old movies or over long conversations, you decided your masterpiece was finished. It sits folded at the foot of your bed now, twice the size of any normal blanket, and twice as full of history and love.

Your second infinite blanket came to you in graduate school. This was your one and only attempt at knitting. It was a wish made of mustard and cranberry yarn, warming stripes that reminded you of red chile and yellow butter melting on fresh-from-the-skillet tortillas. It would keep the darkness away while living in the land of the cold and the gray. Like your school experience, knitting was less forgiving of your mistakes as you fumbled your way through these more sophisticated stitches. There was no do-over like with crocheting. No re-knits to iron out the kinks. Your only option was to start over completely if you lost a stitch or to keep blazing forward, uninhibited by the lack of perfection.

You chose the latter. Looking back had always seemed like a waste, precision seriously overrated. No, you preferred these flaws and holes in your blanket. The better to let bad spirits escape, according to an old legend native to your beloved Southwest, learned from your mother and practiced each time you wound the wooden needles larger than your forearm around each other. Relearned again and again, when your pages came back dripping with micro-aggressions and cultural superiority. Four years down the road, this one was three times the length any proper blanket should be; you had a lot to work through. A lot to conjure. You could almost trail it along the perimeter of your apartment twice over if you wanted, but you'd much rather snuggle into the all-encompassing folds of that comfortably imperfect and utterly complete blanket. What mattered was that things got done. Perfect stitches are for people who don't want to move forward. So much safer to fuss and dawdle over one precious pattern than to allow yourself to create without censor.

You are working on a new one now, this one moving slower than the others. Almost five years in the making and still only a fraction complete. But you want to take your time with this one. A bright turquoise, crocheted in a series of shells. You will always favor the more forgiving stitch, as you have learned the power of generosity and gentleness. It is longer than the others, and it will be the strongest. The most infinite.

It is your New Mexico blanket; each stitch infused with your love of the desert, begun with the intention of weaving together a life you always imagined living. A teacher. A writer. A living story with roots firmly planted in the Land of Enchantment. Yes, this one is still in progress and may always be. There is no rush. You feel no pressure when you set it aside to craft yet another infinite blanket, this one a twin of yours, though it is not for you.

This next blanket is hot pink, a bold sister to your turquoise, and synonymous with your desert aesthetic. A fearless color bound together by those forgiving crocheted shells, so that your niece may live and love and be in the world boldly. This is her blanket. She will know that she is surrounded by warmth and affection conjured from years of her mother and aunts weaving the future together. This is a blanket for the new generation of women in your family. A new generation that, like you and your sisters did together so long ago, will learn the power of the infinite as a series of loops and pearls that spread out behind you in your journey toward the sun.

She will know the power of the infinite.

She will be infinite.

Routine as Ritual

You are nothing without your routine. Some see it as mundane. The petty intricacies of getting through the day. The nails that bind us to a coffin-like existence. But you are nothing without your routine. You need – thrive – on your morning oatmeal made before the sun is up and luxuriate in the quiet hum of words whispering their secrets to your once empty page at the end of the day. Each item of clothing you fold and each dish you wash is a devotional act to living with intention – because you are nothing without your routine.

You mull these thoughts over as you snuggle under a cranberry throw on your porch and cradle a mug of cinnamon-spiced coffee, grateful for your Saturday mornings. The view is stunning. Bright gold and orange leaves litter the ground; the almost naked trees stand in stark contrast to the cloud-blanketed sky; and the still, stone fountain in your courtyard is framed by all of this natural glory. For the first time in several weeks, you can savor the slow unfolding of the day.

The past month has been a study in getting to know this new household: moving and unloading boxes, letting the walls around you grow accustomed to your presence. At night, you lull yourself to sleep by the peculiar creaks and whispers of this place. One day, they will not be so strange. They will be the welcome sighs of your home wrapped snug around you. During the day, you perfume each room with cedar wood and lavender oils – except the kitchen. That, you fill with the scents of your cooking. Eventually, these smells will bind themselves to the walls so that the stories of the previous tenants are just a faint memory in the foundation. Each book tucked into your shelves, each plate stacked away in your cupboards solidifies your presence in this space. These are your offerings to your new home. *Be my sanctuary*, you whisper. *And I will fill you with ink-stained pages and garlic cloves.*

Now you begin the most important task of all: *living* in your dwelling. Filling four walls behind a locked door with the daily routines you have come to miss, like the arms of a lover who has been away too long. You have taken them for granted, you realize. Here is your chance to call that routine back to you and foster new rituals in the process. New homes, after all, require that you build new lenses through which to view your world.

You savor the luxury of being able to return to these seemingly rote tasks as you enjoy your hot coffee and the cool autumnal breeze. The early morning yoga in your living room has become a luxury after weeks of being off your regular self-care regimen. Get used to never rolling up your mat. Here is a promise to honor your body. And you take your time organizing your writing desk, scattering it with herbs and crystals and the blood of your early stories. There is always room in your life for books and words. There is reading to be done and writing, hours spent immersed in stories and imagination before you can turn to tending your cool-weather plants. Even cleaning and laundry have become a meditation on the joys of a warm, clean home.

The weekly grocery store visit is a feast for the senses. You fill your refrigerator with Brussels sprouts, jewel-toned pomegranates, and sharp cheddar, your cabinets with Bordeaux and plump dates. You fill your spice rack with fresh herbs and homemade elixirs. And you cook. The blue corn spinach tart and roasted red chile-spiked butternut squash are for your weeknight meals; the impromptu afternoon tea with your mom made with Earl Grey and a hastily prepared tray of fruit, toast, and jam; and the casual popcorn and hard cider happy hour with your sister – these simple meals invite warmth and love into your home.

Like grooves in a well-trod path, these acts are indulgent rituals of self-care, as rich and filling as your morning brew. You take comfort in the knowledge that when you get home at the end of a long workday your routine is in place – to say nothing of your morning meditations. You water your plants. You walk, eager to converse with the neighborhood trees. You prepare dinner while watching the news and dine listening to old jazz records. You read over cups of raspberry leaf and mint tea. It is a healing balm to a full day of caring for others. It is the promise of soul replenishment and the conscious crafting of an abundant life. You marvel at the rituals you've cultivated over the years to ground you to this earth, and laugh at yourself for taking them for granted while you unpacked boxes and organized drawers. What is routine but a repetition of what you feel your life should – *could* – be?

Happy to be back in your routine, you snuggle more deeply into the warm blanket and take another sip from your mug, now almost empty. Soon it will be time to refill your cup and start breakfast. But there is still time enough to greet the dawning day. Perhaps this is part of your new weekend routine.

On Chamomile

It is the soft yellow heads you see first, then the thin white petals dried into healing slivers. You smell ripe apples and rich earth next, the sweet graininess of the little flower a soothing potion when steeped in hot water. You can recall their midsummer happiness as they flooded your garden path with their heads like daisies and their leaves like fennel fronds. Other times, you are reminded of your first memorable cup of tea, sweetened with honey because you did not yet know the bracing beauty of brewed naked herbs. Even now, a cup of chamomile tea tastes like childhood, apples, and the best kind of medicine.

Gingerly, you gather a small handful of these fragile flowers and funnel them into a tea strainer as wide as your favorite mug, ribboned with stripes and patterns in various colors. The white fringe surrounding the flower's head mimics a starched collar, lending an awkward air of formality to this ground herb. Inside the mason jar where you store them, you see the brittle, straw-like stems and the soft fluff of dried petals make a carpet of cornflower yellow, where the few whole buds nestle, softer than salt through your hands and sweeter too. A fine pollen-like dust sticks to your fingers.

You pour hot water through the strainer and into your mug, enjoying the sweet steam that rises to kiss your face; it is the perfume of sugared grass and sun-warmed fruit lapping over your skin. You watch the flowers bloom anew in your mug, the white petals unfurling and then dissolving into the warm liquid. Unassuming like the dandelion and yet, a potent brew to heal any number of ailments from a throat tightened by things you are too afraid to voice to chaffed skin in need of regeneration. The flowers float and swell in the water, become softer.

When it is time, you remove the strainer from your mug, leaving behind only a thick concoction the color of yellow straw

– your liquid sun cupped between your hands. You take a sip, letting it wash your throat and course through your body, at once attracting abundance and repelling unwanted energies, if lore is to be believed. Just one sip of the brew from this apple-scented flower and you are convinced. Inside and out, it has cocooned your body in its warmth, sheltered you from that which you don't need and saved you for that which you do.

Come spring, you must plant more of these flowers in your garden and in your heart.

On Long Walks

In your experience, there are two kinds of walks: one for adventuring and the other, contemplation. It might seem like splitting hairs to distinguish the difference between what is basically the act of putting one step in front of the other each time you leave your doorstep. They both start the same: a desire to move, to forgo the comforts of home in favor of time among the trees. But where a walk can take you, now that is another thing altogether.

Let's start with the adventuring. That morning you wake up with an expansive feeling in your chest, a longing to roam to the farthest reaches of your territory. You want the sun on your skin and fresh air to tickle your nose, to wander wherever your feet will take you. Perhaps to the neighborhood bookstore, or to the park, full of families playing games and couples walking their dogs. All you know is that you must walk until the bright energy in your chest reaches your toes, and your whole body sings with the fullness of life.

The birds support this plan, luring you out of your home with their playful chatter and accompanying you as you drift through the city, one step at a time. The naked tree branches remind you that it's still winter, although it feels more like the first kiss of spring in the air.

You pause at each street corner to consider your next direction. Flip a coin. Heads you go right, tails left, or forget the coin and zoom on ahead careless of the forks in the road. Your decisions move you toward an unplanned adventure, the promise of an unexpected delight. Even as you move forward, a part of you is waiting expectantly, longing for a joyful surprise hidden behind each turn on your journey, a mystery to be discovered, a hidden gem of something or another to be revealed. Because today, your city is more than just a map of routes that get you from A to B, but a nest of haunts and jewels to be savored, lingered over, like a cup of tea on a cold day.

That is the adventuring walk.

Then there is the contemplative walk. That's the walk that wants only the silence between stirring leaves and time to lose yourself in thought, or to quiet your mind when it sounds louder than the chatter of finches outside your door. This is the walk you crave when there are things to do, tasks to accomplish, which somehow seem so unimportant. You need to leave time for a little soul tending. The contemplative walk calls to you when the afternoon resists work, beckoning you from your perch at your desk, luring you outside to bask under the tender caress of the soft spring sun like a kitten stretched out under a plot of light by the window.

It is fresh air you need. You know that, now that you are walking. The breeze with the faint hint of growing things, the smell of dirt and dry grass and sunlight. You take in one long breath, then another and another, letting your chest expand with this intoxicating air. Gradually, you become aware of other things – the birds singing, finches, doves, sparrows, pleasantly clamoring for attention all at once (now pleasingly louder than your mind, which has fallen into a drowsy hush). You even hear the sharp cries of a hawk as you stroll around the park. You watch people tossing balls with their dogs, children sliding down the playground slides, and others lazily circling the park just as you do. You relish how the sun seems to melt away their cares, and even the normally frazzled soccer mom looks fresh, vibrant with the promise of spring in the air.

With each lap, you admire the homes – especially the tenderly cared for adobes – and the grounded, calm energy they represent. Each tired thought or seemingly heavy chore dissolves under the sun's tender caress and the sight of everyday life going on around you. That knot in the back of your mind – the one about what to write next or how you might find stillness in a world that seems afraid to stop moving – untangles itself as each foot presses its sole against the earth. Soon it is time to wind your way back to your home, the cares of your work left scattered on your desk, all but forgotten by you.

That is the contemplative walk.

In either case, they both end the same. When your legs tire and your appetite is sated, you wander home. Happy with the roaming but happier still to return to your sanctuary, the promise of a hot bath or a glass of wine awaiting you. Your mind is clear, your heart full of sun and the expansiveness of the world around you.

My Joy Is My Resistance

Yesterday I cleaned the house. My home. From top to bottom with elbow grease and burning sage. I tore up disappointments, collected broken hearts for my compost, and laid them to rest among the worms and coffee grinds.

I honor my sacred space because I built it with my own hands and my own dreams. I honor it because they want me to be ashamed of my hard work or collapse under its burden. They don't know that my daily industry is what keeps my fire stoked. That the many hours harvesting seeds has given me a bumper crop of hope and rosemary to chase away unwelcome spirits that come knocking on my door.

I pickled jalapeños, too, because it is nothing short of a minor crisis not to have these green disks warm my belly with their thick seeds. I listened to bachata to warm my heart – and yes, my … well, you know. I even danced in the kitchen, the whisks and spoons and mason jars full of vinegar and jalapeños my dance partners. I danced because there are those who want me broken, not the supple sapling that bends, shakes, and shimmies in the wind.

And my words … not everyone wants me to have them; but the second they take one from me, I just write another and another until the darkness is swept away in the flood of my story. They are afraid of my body, too. My hips and square shoulders and my steady gaze that won't look down. Let them be. Let them quake as I plant my feet firmly into the earth and spread my joy like tree roots underground, perhaps imperceptible, but the foundation for a stronger future.

Let them watch the hope blossoming in my body with each sun salutation and wonder that I sway my hips – those things they wish they didn't want to hold on to – when my heartbeat is the only music. Let them know that I relish the way the sun kisses my bronze skin and keeps me warm when others would stamp out my fire. And when they would try to extinguish my joy, I let laughter bubble from my throat like a thirst-quenching brook.

My hands relish the feel of my dreams being coaxed to life between my fingers like the red clay of my beloved desert and my mother's studio. I mold the clay, and I love the earth, and I shape it into stories they do not want me to tell. The ones of hope. The ones of healing. The ones that remind us of the moon's power and our own capacity for abundance and possibility.

I will take these dreams, and I will swallow them. And I will take these dreams, and I will return them to the earth. And I will take these dreams, and I will offer them up to the sky. And I will make my home in them. Let them burst like rain-soaked seeds fattened by my fertility and the honeyed sweetness of joy.

On Dreaming Deeply

You are craving it. A deep sleep that makes you forget where and who you are and yet brings you closer to yourself. In the hollow between rib cage and stomach, you can feel the weightlessness, almost like motion sickness that has you yearn for the sanctuary of your bedroom and the cottony comfort found within the folds of lavender-scented reveries. Who are those strange creatures, you wonder, who can't – won't – dream? You could never be a night owl. You would miss your dreams too much, as they would miss you.

You welcome sleep with the arms of a lover as you crawl into bed and turn off the lamp. The thick comforter and patterned sheets that hold you are nothing compared to the tender excitement of finally being able to rest your head against plush pillows. Let your eyelids grow heavy now with Morpheus' microscopic sleeping seeds. You wait for him to take you, however impatiently, knowing full well that he will take the time he wants to take. At first, he courts you slowly with fluttering lids and a softened gaze. Then he is upon you all at once, pulling you deeper into a realm beyond your own, while you can still sense your body nestled peacefully under all those blankets.

It is not the sleeping you love as much as the dreaming. You long for the stories that unfold behind your eyelids, and the parts of yourself to awaken that are too often submerged in a hazy half-sleep throughout the day. What you forget each morning when you wake and remember in those moments between lucidity and sleep at night, is that the daylight hours are only half your life, often the least eventful. It is the dreaming hours in which you progress, find solutions to the tangles of your day, remember the spark that reaffirms your path. It is under the watchful eye of the moon that you are allowed to be fully yourself in all versions of your universe.

Deeper still you go, beyond the literal world you left behind in your bed. To places with no names and languages beyond the scope of your wakeful self, but somehow, are intrinsically yours when you give yourself over to Morpheus. His wings give you flight, your own set of feathers protruding from your shoulder blades. It is the dreaming you look forward to, the promise that life is eternal and so often felt in sensations beyond daylight words. So much so, it is a wonder your waking life is not its own dream meant to pass the hours, the minutes until you can once again be claimed by that other place, that other embrace.

Burning Old Man Gloom

Zozobra.

Old Man Gloom. The giant beast of darkness and despair. The decrepit soul eaten up by flames once a year when the sun begins to turn its light from this earth, and we descend into the depths of the inward-turning months. Since 1926, they say. As if you can put a time stamp on such ceremonies.

You know better. You know it is an eternal ritual. A continual exorcism. Though you've never been to the iconic burning in your homeland, nor stuffed the gloom boxes scattered around Santa Fe with your burnable past, you have the knowledge to call up the fire spirits so that they may chase away the gloomies. You have no need for a small wooden tomb to hold your shadows, nor a towering effigy made of chicken wire and dead things, like dry sticks that you wish to forget. Who knew there was so much kindling in the days you've left behind? You could not hold the weight of the many notes you might scrawl throughout the year until the turning leaves gave you permission to stuff them into tin cans and send them to the Old Man. Your fingers would roughen and bleed from the effort of holding on to these regrets. And why would you want to hold them close? So tightly? The things that made them have already served their purpose. You do not need to keep their shadows among your garden steps.

You know better because each and every day you burn Old Man Gloom with your own fire. Your light fuels you and cleanses your spirit from the shades and whispers of doubt that seek to make their home in your skin. You swallow a box's worth of matches, one by one, to start the fire in your belly. Devils be warned, they should stick to the shadows or your light will swallow them up, too.

From time to time, you honor the fire spirits with hot tequila on your tongue and more matches planted in a jagged row like a makeshift fence along the perimeter of your home – but there is no blowing them down. You chase away the daily dreads and feed the gloomies to your hungry lantern, knowing full well you cannot afford to harvest each tattered hope or the frayed bitter corners of your heart, and sit and wait and watch as another feeds them to Old Man Gloom once a year. You must tend your home yourself. Today and every day. Or else those whispers grow so strong, you find yourself keeping house with dust and dead things, seduced by their familiarity like a cloudy blanket. Funny how we fear losing the chains to our past. Funny how we worry and fret about what the unknown might bring. The shadows feed these voices if you surround yourself with gloom boxes.

So you begin your incantation: *Goodbye Old Man Gloom, today and every day. With my light, I banish you. With my light, I banish stagnate energies. With my light, I banish old selves that no longer serve me. With my light, I banish the woe others cast my way. I let the flames of my soul burn them alive until they are nothing but ash and charred bits of history, good for nothing but fuel for my cosmic compost.*

On Belief

There once was a woman who dared to let her thoughts run wild. She lived in a happy adobe at the end of a sunlit road paved by hollyhocks and good cheer. She let these thoughts have free range over her garden and kitchen and through the rest of the rooms in her home. She let them take up space in her heart and watched as they spread like dandelions across her torso. And in return, they filled her with light.

It's a wonder she had so much light.

So much so that I wanted to know her secret. Where did it come from? It seemed to radiate from her as if she were her own sun. And yet I hardly believed her when she gave me the answer.

Here is her truth:

She knew thoughts were the deepest form of magic. She knew we all had the capacity to conjure day after day, crafting our lives through a series of routines, thoughts, actions, and dreams. She knew even a small idea created our reality and would pave the road to our future. It is the strongest yet most ephemeral magic with which she built her home. This thing called belief.

Yes, magic. Often cast without conscious intention, all the more dangerous for its potential lack of clear purpose, it is a well-worn road made by the repeated tread of footsteps. This she told me as she stacked hollyhock seeds one on top of the other to build her porch. But like any magic, you must be careful how you use it. It can be like a shovel you use to dig yourself an eight by three foot box in the earth, flinging dirt and muddy thoughts over yourself once you've climbed down that hole. Or it can be like a seed. *This* seed – she held up a fat black disk to make her point – plunged deep into the earth not to die but to find its purpose in the burst of curly roots pushing into the below and the above.

If not a seed or a well-worn road, let it be a butterfly's wing, so fragile and yet capable of lifting you from the chrysalis. Still not convinced? This she asked me as I marveled at her answer. Then think of belief as the silky wisp of a caterpillar's thread. Breakable with just one limp strand but, over time, when spun with others and wrapped continuously around itself, it becomes a home for the coming transformation. Belief is a supple backbone, flexible and strong as it radiates outward from your core to craft your world from hopes and dreams and fears and what-will-bes and what-might-have-beens and, hopefully, with focused intent. You have no use for graves, only gardens.

Here is a woman who knows some of the strongest seeds are words. The ripest fruit is one delicious thought. I would like to be this woman. No, I correct myself.

I am this woman. I pick up another handful of seeds and continue building.

Descending into the Underworld

You are like Persephone – except you don't regret letting those ruby seeds pass your lips and spill across your tongue. In fact, sometimes you miss the tart, bright taste when the days are long, and the sun tries to remind you that the only thing you should savor is its fingers kissing your spine. And when the days grow shorter and the nights longer, you begin your preparations. You bathe your feet in moonlight and wash your hair in the evening breeze; you lay your plants to rest and store their precious harvest in mason jars. Then, it is without fear that you begin to make your descent into the Underworld.

Not Hell. You've lived there once and know it is not below ground, only in the cold embrace of isolation. Nor is it Milton's proverbial nine layers, though you've traveled those a time or two. It can be hard to remember, but you always think of them when you peel back the layers of an onion. Blessedly, it's not Florence's *Last Judgement* foretelling the heavenly dangers of earthly sin with vicious glee, safety nestled within the bosom of its canonical dome. Something about that mural gives you a taste for vice, despite its dire warnings. What a relief to live an imperfect life!

No, your Underworld is that quiet place which is not a place. A cave below the earth and deep inside yourself. The silent room you retreat to when the world gets too loud, and you have been too long on its surface. You relish the yearly transition from the spring above to the winter below, feeding upon those ruby pomegranate seeds. The stains they leave in your mouth are the price you pay for living both above and below, proof that you are ready to turn away from external revelries. You are bound to this cycle just as Persephone is to hers; you cannot change it any more than she can. Not that you would want to. The earth pulls you into its embrace, thick roots easing your passage into your deeper sense of being, sweeping away the debris of shallow living.

It is there in the quiet and the shadows that you may meditate, contemplate who you are once you've cast off your worldly shell. You will navigate the dark, the shadows of the yet-to-be-revealed; the wisdom to be courted with your solitude. You watch the half-visible figures slowly swirling around you as if they were dancing oracles foretelling your future by the sway of their hips. You gobble up this underground wisdom, as you did those pomegranate seeds, one tiny morsel at a time, feeding your soul. And then – then you rest. You lay your head in the crook of your arms and the roots wind around you, a blanket to keep you warm during your winter-long stay.

Life Is a Celebration

Yesterday, I had a cookout with fresh corn and kebabs on the grill and Django Reinhardt on the record player. Why? Because it was Tuesday and I was hungry. This morning, I did yoga to the sunrise and drank coffee on the patio because that's the best time to talk to the birds and my plants. There was a moment just now, too, where I let my mind wander and breathed in the heady aroma of blue sage because I could.

I am learning not to be too stingy with my enjoyment, you see. Squeezing it in on the weekends. Stuffing myself in a panic as if Monday might steal away my ability to enjoy the world. Rationing it out across each evening, Sundays through Thursdays. Pushing it out of my nine-to-five. I am learning that my supply of joy is not limited, that I don't need to bottle it up or store it in a small jar and tuck it into the back of my pantry for some other day.

That will not do.

On Thursday, I burned an expensive candle and had a glass of even finer whiskey solely because I enjoyed the searing light of fire within and without. There was no point in waiting for a special occasion, whatever that is, like a fence that limits pleasure to some distant future moment. Monday was another story. I drank up the stars late into the night because that was as long as it took to finish my conversation with them. And the blades of grass between my toes today were proof that walking barefoot was as good for my soul as it was for my soles.

I've tasted these honeyed moments and can no longer see the value of life without a backyard bursting with hollyhocks. Enjoyment is too precious a necessity to sit neglected on some dusty shelf. It must be brought into the light and savored every day. I cannot live without that lush, bubbly feeling that tickles my senses like a glass of champagne, getting me drunk on the pure deliciousness of one moment experienced fully. I will not turn away from such bliss, nor wearily resign myself to a stint of a week or a month at more chaste living, as if I were perpetually half-ashamed of my hedonism. I will call to pleasure and search for those pockets of celebration in my day.

Later, I might decide to twirl – in the rain or on the dance floor – for the sheer pleasure of feeling my body move. And I will most definitely lose track of time at some point in the week, let those pesky seconds and minutes dissolve into bliss. Perhaps it will be while reading – no, napping – under a shady tree or swimming in the mellow current of summer. Either way, it will happen on a day just like any other, with no importance to it except that it is today. Or maybe that it is every day, a gentle aroma of fresh mint in the garden, a new book to read, a spontaneous picnic.

And you, you should know that enjoyment is a big-hearted creature, growing bigger, bolder each time you seek her out. She will take over everything if you let her – and you should. Get drunk on the sunset. Let the hum of your daily work wash over you: a rhythm made up of pen on paper, coffee pot, and car engine. Embrace that heady perfume of your dinner cooking on the stove, the lure of a half-finished book on your nightstand. You should even relish the pile of laundry that keeps you home for an afternoon, bringing you back to you.

In any case, tomorrow I will marvel at the host of ladybugs making their home in a broom plant overflowing with tiny yellow flowers. They seem to have found their joy in the thin green stalks they climb upon.

An Unexpected Afternoon Tea

It was nothing fancy. You simply found yourself hungry around three o'clock. You hadn't had lunch. Breakfast had been a long morning affair, keeping you full for quite some time. You still didn't feel like a proper meal. It was too close to dinnertime for that. Still, a little something would be desirable. A small treat to hold you over until dinner.

You coax yourself up from your perch on the patio, laying your reading aside with the promise of something to nibble on as you finish that next chapter. Food and books. Reading and eating – now there are two pastimes that go together admirably. You rummage through the kitchen cupboard, finding nothing to inspire you. The sun-dried tomatoes and canned marinated artichokes feel too much like an evening appetizer, the whole wheat crackers less than inviting. You turn to your refrigerator. Surely there is something there, between your drawers full of vegetables and fruit neatly stacked on shelves. Some quick pickles maybe? Or a slice of toast? And then, your eyes land on it, a cherry empanada from your favorite bakery. How could you have forgotten it?

A plan quickly forms in your mind, and your heart skips a beat at this unexpected pleasure. Afternoon tea on your porch. You heat the water, deciding on an earthy hojicha, a personal favorite whose roasted earthiness will balance out the sweetness of your pastry. You plate your little snack and let your tea steep in your well-used mica teapot. You take your afternoon tea things on a tray to the patio.

As you let your tea finish steeping, you return to your book, feeling not unlike Bilbo Baggins enjoying the comforts of your very own Bag End. You ease back in your chair, ready to enjoy your impromptu tea and the rest of your novel. The empanada is sweet. The tea is strong. The afternoon is perfect.

On Hot Air Balloons

The sun has barely peeked over the purple mountains, as if spraying its golden tendrils across the rocky shoulders of its lover. The air is redolent with the scent of burning cedar from nearby fireplaces, mulched leaves, and the promise of frost. In a word, the morning smells like autumn.

It feels as if only you and the frost are awake.

Your car engine rumbles to life, and you ease into the slip-stream of the half-asleep city streets. That's when you first spot a floating dream out of the corner of your eye. A remnant of last night's lucid voyages, there in the distant horizon. On the other side of town, where the sky meets the earth, there is no mistaking it. A hot air balloon. The first of many, releasing themselves into the sky, happy to be rid of the weighty ropes that tethered them to the earth.

This one is full and fat with yellow and red stripes like those of a circus tent. It looks so small from your vantage point near the mountains, clear across the other side of the city, as if it were an ornament or earring dangling on a hook from a stray cloud. Yet you know they can be bumbling monsters up close.

They might coast too near your car in traffic-clogged streets or fall apart in your backyard, all heaps of unruly silk and coils of rope. But that is only because their home is in the sky, and like any winged creature, they do not know quite what to do with themselves when they touch the ground. You cannot expect them to enjoy the way the earth can cradle them when they come undone. Not as you relish the ground cupping your feet when you want no other company than the dirt between your toes and the firm hold on your spirit when you feel as if it might drift away.

Still, you admire these tributes to whimsy, kept afloat by nothing more than invention and imagination. You have often wondered what it would be like gliding across the earth in a four by four wicker basket – or so you always presume the dimensions to be, a byproduct of reading adventure novels and loving old things – guided by the changing winds and a desire to see the world from a new perspective. Not much different from your life on land then.

Even so, it would be something to sail from horizon to horizon, or as you often dream, to another world. One of wonder and imagination, waiting just beyond the seam where the earth and the sky meet in the distance. You want to slide your finger across the picture perfect line that separates earth from sky, dip your finger into all that possibility.

You want to wander and remember what it is like to be weightless. You want to find yourself wrapped in a yellow and red striped hug. You want to be the promise of adventure on the horizon before the day sweeps everything away.

On Home

It is your sanctuary.

Your refuge from the world, all that bustle and noise. The quiet place where you rest the mind and nourish the soul. The only place where you can safely peel back the layers of the day until all that is left is freshly scrubbed elbows and knees. Tender skin exposed. Breathing freely now that you've cast off your thicker skin. Your armor sags on a hanger in the back of your closet, waiting to be donned again the next day.

Home is more than just a place to sleep, more than just a few rooms to dump your belongings. What heartbreak it would be to come home to an empty husk of a place with no soul at all. Instead, you have built this home out of antique furniture and what you imagine your dream adobe should be like. Everything is art, each soup bowl or coffee table not just there for necessity but pleasure. The haphazard stack of old books and meticulously cultivated crystal collection add warmth and beauty to your refuge. You want to feel the luxury of your senses being saturated by wonderful things.

You ponder this as you slide your key into the front door, so grateful for the coming hours of solitude. The inside smells faintly of pineapple and sage, a byproduct of the fruit ripening in a ceramic bowl on the kitchen counter and weekly smudging to cleanse your space of negative energies. You take one breath then two, inhaling that Pavlovian scent that tells you the day is done. There is joy, too, in taking in the sight of all your familiar things. The fat mica tea mug left just so in the kitchen sink waiting to be washed. The small green colander overflowing with squash and two tomatoes – the foundation for your evening meal. Or the dish towel freckled with lemons that bring a smile to your face whenever you look at it.

Your gaze drifts farther past the kitchen to the living room.

Your work in progress, a turquoise knitted blanket, is dumped haphazardly on your ruby couch, left from the night before when you were too tired to fold it before bed. Then there is the rolled yoga mat leaning against the corner of your bookshelf, an open invitation to be spread out and danced upon...if you don't get distracted perusing your stuffed bookshelf first.

These things, *your* things, they are your home. They fill up your space with memories of collecting seashells on the Californian and Italian shores, of books read and reread. Each book never giving you the same story twice as life experience seasons your understanding of what makes stories worth telling, worth reading. The warmth in your kitchen, the result of a well-worked stove and long family dinners. Your bedroom is a riot of color and crystals hanging from your wall. This room above all others is where you can fully shed your outer shell – that prim teacher who always needs to be respectable – and allow yourself the grace of hair loose around your shoulders and bare feet and an uncensored heart.

Here, too, you soak up the love carved from the art on your wall and photographs of those you hold dearest, the only ones you have room for in your life. You wrap these memories, these imprints of time around you, like a hug that squeezes out the last remnants of your daily performance just as you wipe the last bit of makeup from your face. There you are, looking back at yourself from your antique vanity piled high with old perfume jars and, yes, more crystals (memories too). There is the one that craves solitude at the end of a long day and nothing more than a good jazz record to read by.

There you are. Covetous of this space like a secret held in the palm of your hand. Here is your dream adobe tucked behind four unassuming apartment walls and deep within your heartbeat.

Cooking an Onion

Ah yes, dinner.

You don't know what you feel like and, at the end of the day, are incapable of making any real decisions. But you know just as well that you must eat. Wine only gets you so far. So you turn to a kitchen ritual so old you don't remember who you learned it from. Your mother, most likely, or perhaps your Florentine sister teaching you yet another Italian custom. In any case, you know what must be done.

You need to cook an onion.

The culinary Oracle. Once gently simmering in your pan, the onion will divine the future of your kitchen table. This bulb will wake up your palate and reveal that which you most desire – for tonight, anyway. Cooked in ghee or olive oil, the softening skin of this sweet yellow offering will tempt you with the promise of sautéed kale and roasted sweet potatoes, or perhaps a hearty stew that simply needs celery and carrots to complete the base. There is only one way to find out.

So you deftly move through your conjuring ritual with the ease of someone who has done it often. You pull a sweet onion from your cupboard and lovingly chop it up on your cutting board. The tears burn your eyes: a sacrifice to this bulbous Oracle. The salt running from your face will season the skillet and the steam that rises from it will reveal your dining future. If you're lucky, it will evaporate any sadness you had not known you carried.

Onion tears are like that, plucking grief from the shadows of your heart. There's no hiding from an onion. You heat up your olive oil as your tears season the pan, feeling somehow lighter, though you didn't know you had been carrying the burden now lifted from your shoulders. You enjoy the pop and sizzle as you slide your second, more tangible offering to the culinary powers that be into the pan.

There is nothing left to do but let that humble kitchen staple begin to caramelize. Sometimes you stir the slices as if prodding them to reveal their secrets. Sometimes you drink wine. Sometimes you marvel at the dried tearstains on your cheeks. The Oracle speaks in its own time. You wait for that moment of inspiration as patiently as your grumbling stomach will allow. You feel the pungent scent of this earthy root drift through your home, conjuring up memories of comforting meals like ratatouille or roasted vegetables. But it is dahl that finally calls to you. Cooked to perfection, once the onions are added to the lentils along with garlic and cumin. Yes, dahl, finished off with a heaping tablespoon of catharsis and fresh winter vegetables.

The Oracle has spoken.

To Be Still

Pause when your bow kisses the violin's strings. Resist the temptation to slide rosin-dusted horsehairs across ribbed metal. Hold the moment inside you like a delicious dream from the night before. Fingers gently tease the frog; chin and shoulder hug the fragile wooden vessel while your other hand cradles its neck. The music will come soon enough. For now, the beauty is in the stillness.

There are no wrong notes or a skittering bow sliding sloppily across A and D strings. There is no perfect vibrato. No effortless use of the fourth finger across your E string (the hardest to reach, but more delicious than honey on toast when your pinky presses against the thin chord's sweet spot). The pleasure is anticipating the unfolding song, blessed mistakes and unintended miracles and all.

Let that pause remind you of your breath. Where had it gone? You feel it now, allowing your ribcage to expand and contract with each tender inhale. Take this stillness into your day. Bottle it up like you might rosin dust or the stray notes of a new song. Hold on to it when you would want to fill your head with deadlines and dandelion heads. Though you suppose the dandelion heads aren't so bad. And resist the temptation to fill your basket simply because it is empty. No – not empty. You can see now how the supple wooden arms bend and fold around one another, cradling their own potential. Just admire the way nature has braided itself into an embrace and ignore the pull to make yourself useful.

Find your footing, the stillness says. Feel the way the ground presses against the pads of your feet as if to hug them forever. Let go of the need to run. The ragged motion only keeps your soles from this earth. Pull back from the ever-spinning carousel that so dizzies you and experience the blades of grass slipping between your toes, the scent of rain in the air. Allow yourself to feel your own song. The murmured melody pulsing in your veins.

Hold yourself there. Acquaint yourself with the pads of your feet and their high arches upon which you rest before taking the next dance step. Become comfortable with the space you have created for silence (that most elusive of creatures, hardest of all to find and keep) before the melody sweeps you away in a flurry of congas and drums. And when your feet move, don't let them run but shift and sway in conversation with the Earth beneath them. Let the breeze quiet your mind and sweep away the temptation to hurry off somewhere else. There is no need; it will remind you time and time again. Your happiness is right here in the tranquil silence between each breath.

Soon you will swoop your bow down across violin strings with vigor; soon your hips will sway and shimmy with every ounce of joy held tight in your body, relishing the fullness that emerges after you have filled your cup with the heady song of silence and the delectable dance of stillness.

But for now, make your home in possibility.

Grocery Lists

A little black chalkboard sticks to your refrigerator door. Four inches by six framed by wood, dented and scraped from two moves and time. The face is dusty and faded with white chalk smudges. You write *basil* in your customary scrawl to remind yourself that you need to whip up some peace and pesto, and then *onions,* for you seem forever in need of grounding and have just used the last sweet bulb in the pantry.

Those onions simmer in the pan, readying themselves for your favorite caramelized onion and mushroom pizza and filling your kitchen with their savory aroma. You take a moment to wipe the chalk from your hands and admire this grocery list. *Bell peppers* is still faintly visible behind cloudy, half-erased smudges along with *olives* and *eggs*. You warm at the thought of yellow yolks making their home inside your belly and the way briny olives taste like sea-soaked sunshine in your mouth.

There is a blank space over *blue corn tortillas*, those kitchen staples you have had on your list for some time. The one item you keep forgetting to pick up with each trip to the grocery store. All those thoughts of olives remind you that you are running low on olive oil, so you add that to the list. You cannot be without that green liquid, a blessing across your skillet. And because you always need quality coffee, you add that to the list too. Better to have more than you think you need than to wake up one morning wanting for a cup of the good stuff. List updated, you wipe your hands on your apron before returning to the task of slicing mushrooms.

It occurs to you as you finish caramelizing your onions that your life is made up of a series of grocery lists, each one building off the other, like layers of paint on an artist's canvas. Better still, no grocery list looks the same. Each stroke is the promise of a weekend feast, or a simple weeknight meal, or a kitchen experiment that makes no promises to its edible outcome. Your life is made up of late night, post-dancing nibbles and red wine, morning chia seeds and fresh blackberries, and those lamentably forgotten blue corn tortillas. Each stew is a nutritious potion infused with only the best intentions. Each slice of toast slathered in ghee and refrigerator jam, an edible memory of quiet spring mornings or boisterous afternoons running outside, shaking off the numbers and lessons and the sit-stills of the day. There is tranquility in the soft embrace of the chile-patterned apron (a gift from your mother) and wisdom in the alchemy of the stove.

It is your daily work of art, and if anyone asked, you would tell them this truth: To know the woman you must look to her pantry. Here a wedge of aged cheddar, there, more radishes because you can never keep enough of them in your refrigerator or your belly. You are a sucker for their peppery bite and red faces. Spinach, your perennial favorite, never quite erased from your list because you always need the taste of green iron in your mouth. There, the jar of sun-dried tomatoes because in the heart of winter, you will need to remember what ripe summer afternoons taste like. And whiskey because a little liquid fire never hurt anybody and the sweet burn of purification is good for the soul.

You eye the bottle on the shelf, only a quarter full of amber liquid. Better add that to the list too, along with bay leaves and the matchsticks you will use to breathe life into your edible conjurings.

A Conversation with Coyote

Yesterday, Coyote paid you a visit.

You first noticed his presence when the street signs disappeared. First they were there clear as day. Then gone. He must have been following you for some time, you realized. But in your haste to get where you were going, you didn't fully take in the telltale prickling of the skin on the back of your neck, as if someone was breathing right behind you, too close and smelling of sage and sweat. Of course, that meant he'd had his eye on you for a while, probably from the moment you stepped outside your home today. He is playful like that. And tricky. He likes to stalk his prey and see how long it takes her to notice his presence.

He must have gotten bored waiting for you to notice him, though. Otherwise, he wouldn't have taken away the street signs. The road stretched out unendingly before you. You had been driving down to the Westside, that strange amalgamation of glorious petroglyphs and clapboard housing, for a Very Important Meeting. You had left early. Worn a sharp outfit. Memorized the careful directions; all in an attempt to make the Best Possible Impression. Everything was going fine until you crossed the river, the Bosque's cottonwoods standing sentry along the bridge and signaling your descent into what would become Coyote's playground.

Still, you had no notion of his presence. You turned on Unser, cruising past the petroglyphs into the wide open expanse of the desert. But the open space did nothing to cure your tunnel vision. You had to get to The Meeting. The road seemed to stretch on forever, and you couldn't seem to find the right turn-off. That is when you noticed the absence of street signs. You had forgotten how much he loves disorder. Or better put: how much he likes to shake up *your* order.

You kept driving, a slow sense of unease bubbled up inside

of you. All the while, you felt rather than heard the pitter-patter of Coyote's feet trailing after you. Saw the telltale signs of his paws muddying up your sense of direction. You drove past one Walgreens after another, one housing development after another, until all the Westside blended together in a stream of buildings built overnight. Eventually, you even lost those. And your last chance to turn back.

Any inkling of civilization was left behind, and you found yourself on a one-lane road driving deeper into the desert, the mountains ahead of you the only witness to your useless sense of direction. You had never seen this part of the city before. You weren't even sure you were still in Albuquerque. Perhaps you weren't. It was as if you stumbled across a lone stretch of land, invisible to all in the city except for those willing to get a little lost once in a while.

It was only when you reached the end of the road – literally a dead end in the middle of nowhere – that Coyote finally revealed himself. The Meeting had already started. Your smart power dress wilted under panic sweat and the desert heat. You would've searched for better directions if your phone could've gotten a signal. Not that it would have helped. Coyote wanted to talk. And when he talked, you listened if you knew what was good for you. Abandoning hope for your Good Impression, you resigned yourself to a conversation with Coyote.

So much for Very Important Meetings.

You stepped outside your car and breathed in the early morning air. The mountains were like sleeping giants at the other end of the metropolis, that sense of order and civilization you now long for. Coyote lurked just behind your bumper, waiting for you to come to him in those last few steps after he had chased you across the city. It was the least you could do. His tongue was fat and lolling from the side of his mouth, his ears long and sharp against the open sky. You leaned against the trunk of your car and folded your arms.

Okay Coyote, you tell him. *I'm listening.*

Then you settled in for a talking to.

He chased his tail and danced around you; his paw stirred up dirt that coated your once perfectly polished heels. He cackled at his own jokes, especially the ones about your now limp hair ready to fall from its up-do. He rolled upon the earth and took no notice of your crossed arms. And then, he stopped. He sat. And he gazed out across the expansive desert before you.

There, alone with Coyote in the middle of the desert, it hit you: You needed to be more than a Very Important Meeting. You needed to let go of the narrow directions, the narrow road you held on to so tightly only minutes before. You needed to let yourself be sand and stone, air and light, mountain and breath, the silence and the drone of cicadas. You needed to be the ribbon of a dirt road that goes everywhere and nowhere. You needed to be the dust settling around your feet. In that moment, you stopped trying so hard. When you looked down beside you, Coyote was gone.

You got back in your car and pulled back onto the road. This time, you found your destination easily. You had passed it some time ago, in fact, not recognizing it for what it was. Of course, missing street signs might have had something to do with that. No matter. It was more important to drive into the desert to have a conversation with Coyote. He would be back, eventually, when your mind got too tight and your view too narrow. But for now, you enjoyed the pleasure of finally reaching your destination – now no longer so very important – however late, however wrinkled your clothes.

You shook your hair loose of its insufferable bun and smiled faintly at the scent of sage and sweat in the air.

Early Morning Yoga

The world is not up yet.

It is only you and the sliver of moon against a pale sky dusted with a few stars, the last holdouts against the coming dawn. The yoga mat is a six-by-two sanctuary. Your breath mingles with the cool breeze floating through an open window. It is time to begin.

You are careful at first, listening for the little snaps and pops of joints, shaking the last tendrils of the dream world from your mind. You feel your way through sun salutations one inhale-exhale at a time, gently courting the golden morning light before it has fully woken, before *you* have fully woken. You coax it out of bed as you coax yourself from the warm covers with the promise of clean energy. You unwrap this gift in the morning devotion to Earth, to sun, to life. Already you feel the lightness of the day beginning to creep into your bones, a luminous experience that will carry you through the rest of the day.

Each morning, the body is different. Today it is slow-moving. You relish the way the spine elongates in the first downward dog of the day, feeling palms and heels press against the mat, fingers and toes splayed. You will stay here awhile; linger in the weightlessness of this pose. Other times, your body is a sunflower ready to burst from the bud, needing the swift, sinuous movement of a vinyasa flow so it can pump blood through its veins. Each day is a new dance, a delicate tango of lunges and bends and twists. The mat is your dance partner, allowing you to sink into the rhythm of your body. You want to know each vertebra as it stretches and lengthens, aligning itself. Your breath is a soft symphony that greets the day, reminding you that you are alive. Each day, you gently peel the moon from your skin and wrap the sun around you. The heat of this exchange, the fire that fuels your day.

It is your moment for you. Your moment to remember that you are body as much as mind before the sun rises, the world begins to move, and you get swept up in the current of life.

On Being an Amateur

You had simply wanted to take a dance class again. Feel the smooth wood floor under your feet as you twirled. And then, the pressure started. You must become a Bronze at the very least. Preferably a Silver or most especially, a Gold. Mastery was a must, though you doubted the lovers dancing in the moonlight cared about missteps that only brought them closer.

All at once, you felt like the young girl who lost her taste for ballet. All you had wanted then was to wear a pink tutu and your hair in a honey bun (the name for your coils wrapped around each other given to you by your mother). And twirl. Always wanting to spread your arms and spin your legs so the world would become a pinpoint of light, and you could feel the heady sensation of being a dandelion wisp whisked through the sky.

This must be what the wind feels like when it whips through trees and tickles flower heads. You had no room for point shoes or bleeding toes. You wanted only to wrap yourself in a cloud of pink tulle and Chopin, just as you now dance to be reminded – absolutely need to remember – that you are a body and a heart and a woman.

When, you wonder, did it become impossible simply to twirl?

Then, there is your home apothecary, though it hardly deserves the word in some circles. Jars of herbs and dried things that get mixed into teas, infused into salves, and poured into bottles. No training, just a desire to feel your garden inside your body. Or the blankets you've crocheted out of half-stitches and unbridled enthusiasm, until someone explained to you that you hadn't used real stitches at all, let alone a discernible pattern. No matter. They still made a blanket. Several, in fact. Imperfect, passable blankets. What more could a woman ask for?

And you no longer care about folding into yourself on the yoga mat so that you are the equivalent of an origami crane surrounded by a thick cloud of incense and sounding gongs. You are a woman, just a woman, who needs only know the pleasure of a quiet morning flow, birdsong her only soundtrack, the sky her only witness to enlightenment – if you could ever use such a lofty word for the act of learning yourself. It's no use ironing out all the wrinkles or fixing every smudge. You would rather twirl. Outside, in the sunlight, grass beneath your feet.

Simply twirl.

On Being an Expert

Syllables. Consonants and vowels. The whole alphabet and the language it breeds through a simple arrangement of letters. Punctuation. Ideas. And those rough and slippery indefatigable belongings we can barely hold on to, and yet they keep a firm hold on us: emotions. These are the things I know.

The inside of a book: glue, thread, pulp beaten and dried until it is a fine sheaf waiting to be touched. Better still, the consonants and vowels strung together to make up the words that get scribbled inside it. I know the taste of a good story as I know the worn edges of a well-loved hardback. More than that, the spark that can only be ignited when dark pen touches virgin paper and the narrative is born. Listen to the story's heartbeat. It will tell me where it wants to go. How it wants to unfold. I must only trust the spilled ink and the scratch of nib on pulp.

And the way it touches me. Not many know the silky feel of words fanning across shoulder blades and trickling down my spine to pool in-between my legs. There is more truth in the distilled liquid of a well-told tale than in any attempt at rational thought.

This I know.

Tasting the First Tomatoes from Your Garden

There they are. Two small cherry tomatoes ripening on your potted tomato plant. Sometime between when you left for your short trip and the time you returned to tend your garden, those little globes went from green peas to ripe red fruit. You stare at them for a long time, not quite believing your luck. Two whole tomatoes, there for your enjoyment.

Barefoot and holding your watering can in one hand and dead plant leaves in the other, you consider your options. You are hesitant to eat them all at once but can't think of any recipe that would call for just two cherry tomatoes. Even worse, you would hate for them to get lost in a salad where the lettuce, vinegar, and olive oil might overwhelm them completely. As you weigh your options, you know you've already made up your mind. You lack the self-control to do anything but eat them straight from the vine. You set your watering can down and toss out your weeds and debris. The rest can wait.

As you pick those little tomatoes, you can feel their sun-warmed skins, the smooth, soft flesh wrapped tautly around their juicy core. You take the first one in your mouth. Allow it to roll around your tongue, almost afraid to break the surface of its skin with your teeth, but you do it anyway. You can't resist the taste of a real tomato.

You feel the skin break, spilling out soft seeds and flooding your mouth with the sweet taste of summer: sun, soil, savory red fruit. You are left with the tart taste on your lips and soil on your hands. It is over too fast; you promise to make the second one last longer but you know it, too, will be gone sooner than you would like. Already your tongue is missing the bright taste of this homegrown magic.

You pop the last one into your mouth, determined to savor

every last inch of it. You roll it around your tongue, remembering why garden tomatoes have turned you against their mealy store-bought cousins. This second one is gone in a flood of seeds and juice. You gaze longingly at your tomato plants, searching for signs of yellow flowers or little green bulbs that will one day ripen into edible euphoria. Until then, you can only wait, water, tend. You pick up your watering can once more and go about the business of tending your garden, the tang of the first tomatoes of the season still fresh on your lips.

A Love Letter to Summer Monsoons

You quiet my mind as you feed the earth. The strength of your thunder, the flash of your lightning all serving to soothe the storm inside me. Your rain kisses my skin, filling the cracks and crinkles of my parched mind as it soaks into the dark soil grounding my plants, burrowing deep into their roots even as it licks their upturned faces.

You send a hush over the city, muting the traffic and day-to-day bustle. All is silenced. You wind your way to your fullest expression, clouds gathering in force behind you, a welcome promise of a deceptively quiet evening within the folds of your wicked embrace. I watch those dark clouds race across the horizon, punctuated by your low grumble that warns the land of your strength, inviting the day to bow before your might. There will be no late night stargazing or reading on the porch. Instead, windows are securely fastened, doors tightly closed. Inward I must go. While the storm rages outside, I smell only the scent of rain on dry earth; hear only drops dancing on my roof.

Your crackle and light soothe me to sleep late at night, the downpour of rain finding me in my dreams. I would run out and dance in you, if I could, if it weren't for the thunder and lightning. Instead, I content myself with listening to your wild symphony. The only noise that can draw me away from my book and my place on the couch, to simply stare out the window and marvel at the song that is my summer monsoon, my healing balm that washes over my soul.

On Wild Hair

Your hair simply can't control itself.

Twice a year you try to tame it – *snip snip* with scissors, *woosh woosh* with the blow dryer, the rounded brush clawing through the kinks and tangles until they are smooth perfection. It pleases you enough to ignore the muttered comments about your coarse ethnic hair and the suggestion of permanent hair straightening treatments for people with my "condition" from the pale woman in charge of disciplining it. Though in truth, her tip might not be so big now. For a few days, you have Movie Hair. Or more accurately, the hospital corners of hair. Each strand is just so, nothing out of place, everything pleasantly unremarkable.

But it's not your real hair. More like that button-up shirt that isn't your style. The one you talked yourself into buying on the assumption that it *might* be you, that one day you *could make it work*. Sometimes you even put it on, just in case today is the day you will like button-up shirts, and know full well it isn't and never will be. The proof is in that shirt crumpled and abandoned on the floor after five unbearable minutes of feeling all those plastic discs pressing against your ribcage and stomach. How does anyone breathe so corseted?

You can't take the flawless hair anymore either. It's too much to live up to, or rather, too much to be contained by. So you turn to your homemade rosemary and olive oil shampoo. It will free your tresses from their prison. From the artificial sprays and pomades that keep your locks reined in. You watch the hospital corners slide down the drain. Feel your wet, thick hair tangled between your fingers.

No more Movie Hair. No, your hair is a riot of half-formed curls and twists that never quite commit to being corkscrew ringlets or soft waves. They colonize your head with a thicket of spirals going in whatever direction they want to. Yours is a wild nest of onion scapes, or the tangle of morning glories creeping through your garden. Like your thoughts that resist linear paths, your hair seeks out the kinks in the road. They are the most interesting part of a story anyway.

These coarse – no, your lips curl at the term, knowing it for the derogatory implication that it is – these strands thick as the roots that bind you to this land, abhor toxic hairspray and little cheap barrettes that try to contain it. The last clip that tried to hold it back snapped in the middle of dinner, sending the tumble of curls over your face and the offending accessory shooting across the room. That was the last time you wore any formal fastener. Your hair rebels against too much product and not enough down time. Even when you coax it into a sophisticated up-do for work, once home, it practically pushes the pins out of its sultry coils.

It will not let you be anything but you. And when you look at it first thing in the morning, a wild riot of auburn curls half-smashed from hugging the pillows all night, you realize that this is you. You are your loud curls that don't like to be contained. Your thick hair that is more comfortable naked and loose than tamed into politeness with sticky pomades you don't know how to properly use, or with that hair straightener that has never left its original box. Those hours spent primping are better spent in your garden. This massive mane of yours cannot be controlled, and you realize as you finally wash out the last of the hospital corners, that you don't want it to. You are bare feet and uncombed curls. Rich roots curling up to the sky above you and down into the earth below you. Wild thoughts and wild hair.

Everyday Conjuring

I burned a bay leaf last night with hopes I could not voice written on its fine-veined underbelly. I fed the ashes to my compost and had the satisfaction of knowing that the moon had heard me. That the stars conspired to birth that wish, born from longing and a pain so sharp I only let myself feel it when wrapped in the silvery healing light of the moon's caress. *Your home is in stardust and tea leaves,* it reminded me. *Not the shallow box you used to fence yourself in.*

I lit beeswax candles to read by, letting my home be filled with the amber scent of honey and healing. There is sweetness in this world, and I would do well to remember that. My dinner was roasted burdock root over a bed of dandelion leaves: a purification spell. Grounding. Detoxifying. The dandelion's sharp flavor expelling the bitterness from my soul, and the soft, sun-ripened burdock root filling the ensuing emptiness with earthy light. *Let it go,* the earth's wisdom whispered. *Let it go and find the seeds of sunshine blossoming in its wake.*

I scattered flowers and crystals across my bedroom so that I may know the finer, softer things in life. So that I may taste soft lips pressed against my skin, like the rose petals that fall, float, and kiss my nightstand with their coy perfume. I let the crystals magnify that potential and fill my room with it. All this, so that one day, I will wake with the knowledge that it is not just me and the rose petals in my bed.

And now: a pinch of nettle leaves. A teaspoon of tulsi. Three slivers of rosemary needles. A hefty scoop of fuzzy chamomile heads and the fruity heart of half a rosehip. Blend in mortar. Funneled into mother's teapot. Flood with hot water and let sit. Pour into mica mug. Drink. Read future at the bottom of the cup, told through a series of unfurled nettle leaves and chamomile petal threads. Feel the future written in the brew now filling my body. Threading through my veins.

    I taste bay leaf ash and a hope finding its home.

A Love Letter to Pleasure

I don't quite understand you.

It is as if you are a word in a foreign language that I can't completely wrap my mouth around. I try desperately, willing my tongue and tonsils to coax the song across my palate with grace, so that one day I may pass as a native speaker of your bliss. So please, have patience with my fumbling. Allow me to take you in, just once more, so that I may know your fullness.

Let me court you. Overlook my uncouth attempts at seduction. Instead, try to be drawn in by my whispers and fluttered eyelashes, though surely they are not as tempting as your sighs and tickles. Or the way you put my life into perspective with a playful shrug of your shoulder. All at once, my too-hot flame becomes a joyful spark under your soothing caress. Remind me, when I stumble, that release is a skill best cultivated through rigorous, delicious practice.

You are Coyote, tempting me off the straight and narrow, that dull anemic path that leaves nothing but an empty cup and a heavy soul. *Okay then*, I say, when you cross my path. *Let's go. Let's get lost in the desert, drunk on the stars, dizzy with the moon.* I won't even pause to catch my breath or search my dictionary to make sure I have the right words for you. They will come on their own. I must trust in that. I must – will – trust that the words, like so many ohs and ahs, will find me.

Yes, you can kiss me, though I hope you would, even without my permission. Or rather, you will always find me open and willing, if awkward. Sometimes I have trouble getting out of my own way, your blustery passion the only thing that reminds me I am a woman with touchable skin and tender ears. That's what makes you the bottomless glass of bubbly or the fleeting scent of lilacs in spring.

And I will reach for you in return, seduced by your mercurial touch. Seduced by the way you make me jealous of a teacup's rim when you press your lips to it or the fortunate nest of morning glories when you weave your fingers through their thick vines. Would that it were my hair, loose around my shoulders, because you – we – like it that way. I will let my body be the earth, and you can be my gardener. Even you, a seemingly flighty creature, have a way of bringing both the lightness of a summer's night and the weight of roots grounding garden herbs into my bones. Let me know the heaviness of you pressed against me. The softness of your breath against my neck.

I need you. And though I know you've heard this before from countless others, on hundreds of other rendezvous, know this: You are my necessity, my home. You bring wings to my discipline and joy to my focus. You are my rosebud, my compass.

What Writing Looks Like

I am lost in thought.

The handful of oregano reminded me of the opening scene of my current story. There is oregano there too. And bell peppers, onions, and tomatoes from the garden. I am no longer in my herb patch but in the kitchen of a home that only exists within the puddles of ink gathering on the page. The people inside the kitchen are making a pizza to cook in the horno that sits at the center of their backyard. They haven't revealed their names yet, just their love of homegrown nourishment and the seed of conflict. Every good story needs one, as much as the soothing crackle of kindling as they ready the oven. *Robert Julian James Luis Luisa Linda Roberta Rosemary* ... and I'm back in my garden again, fingernails lined with dirt. Their names will come in time. *Thyme.* That would go well with my sauce.

I am just a woman gardening. I am just a writer, weaving a story from oregano, eggshells, and a spark of imagination. Casual onlookers do not know that what they just witnessed was nothing short of magic. Perhaps one day they will, though, when they pick up that story with that opening scene in that kitchen built of words and paper and thyme (and more time). Then they will know how I spun stories out of stolen moments among my plants.

Or take the hour I spent away from my writing desk because my body no longer wanted to sit still but dance the silent dance of yoga asana, freeing the words nesting at the bottom of my spine. My prose came more fluidly after that, as if my spinal cord were a pen dipped into the ink of the day, ready to release the stories it had absorbed between sunrise and sunset.

Sometimes my writing is the evening I set aside for more words, but after a day of being saturated in them, I find that there is nothing more appealing than pajamas, a glass of wine, and whatever old movie is playing on the television. And if my hands must move – that twitch, a phantom ache from not pressing fingertips to keyboard – I will knit memories into the threads looped together for my infinite blankets.

Then there are the words hastily scribbled on a crumpled tissue or old handout as my students pore over their marked-up papers, trying to make sense of the narrative I wove into those tight margins. This is when the words come most of all. It is the space between breaths, when I am not allowed to labor over this comma or that scene but can only hastily record a brief flash of insight onto the wilted edge of last month's essay prompt.

And yes, sometimes I even find myself writing at my desk, as people so often suspect I do. I lay sentences, like bricks, into the walls that make up the home of my craft. This comes with its own pull to wipe away the excess mortar from between those bricks. In this, you search for the most elusive of miracles. A page without typos, if such a thing exists. I often wonder, when I run my fingers between my bricks, once again hoping to smooth out the pebbles in the thick cement my hand had already combed through.

More often than not, writing is in the moments I close my eyes and let sleep take over. Where else would I find the worlds carved into the inside of a star, or the memory that seems to come from nowhere except the amber-leafed shade tree I find only at the crossroads between wake and sleep? Other times, I find myself in similar dream worlds, this time within the folds of book covers rather than under my sheets. Yes, my writing is in feeding my soul; each story I devour becomes a future bone in the vertebra of my own.

I find my words, too, at the tip of a fountain pen, waiting to spill its black seed onto my page. Sometimes I keep those seeds in the pen, for as eager as they are to make their mark on this world, I can tell they are not truly ready to commit themselves to paper. This moment between holding my pen and pressing its tip to a blank page is where the writing happens. What stories will ask to bloom before the ink spills?

So I let my words come to me of their own accord. I let myself feel the craft wrap around me like a cozy sweater, stocking up on all those images and feelings and memories – some my own, some pressed within the pages of books – until my pen is full to bursting, ready to let the abundance of my prose gush onto the page. In the meantime, I get lost in thought. I make a cup of tea. I finish that thyme-infused sauce. I take a long walk down a forgotten lane. I feed my senses until I feel as if I might burst with the pleasure of peeling and eating an apple.

Then the story follows.

The Bookshelf

You find yourself gazing at this six-tiered monster, three cases wide, stuffed full of stories with no plan, no pattern. You used to be so careful with your books and their placement. Once they were arranged alphabetically, once by height. Another time by theme, here the epic fantasy series, all the books stacked together in one fat row, and there, the collection of poems, next to your Victorian women authors. You went so far as to separate your hardbacks from your paperbacks once, but that formality didn't last long.

They sit squished together, Victorian authors with the sword and sorcery, the poems mixed in with your cozy mysteries amidst knick-knacks and treasures, just as your sister haphazardly stacked them when she unpacked them from their moving boxes. Now you cannot look upon your shelves without seeing them as another sister memory sewn into the wild literary forest mapped by these piled books. Yes, these precious books, collected over the years, are stuffed into each shelf like paper sardines. You almost do not have enough room, so your books must shed their modesty and take up house with a kaleidoscope of other words. Yet you cannot make yourself bring order to this joyful chaos.

You wonder what they have to talk about, the Colette novels that kiss your collection of fairy tales and hold up your cheesy romances written in Spanish. You wonder, too, if those stories begin to bleed into one another with their covers pressed so tightly against each other. Here no genre is favored, no era, nor any one writer. Your leather-bound books, tinted with nostalgia and the heady perfume of history, keep house with beat-up pulp paperbacks, their covers splashed with blush-worthy tableaus. Over time, each story has bled through its cover and seeped into the sheaf of ink-stained papers on either side of it. They must, for how else are new stories made? How else do you account for that slim paperback appearing sandwiched between two other books, holding a story you never knew existed, let alone purchased?

Your bookshelf seems to sigh and settle under the weight of so many stories upon its back, piled between its wooden bones. The knick-knacks strewn across these fleshy piles are road signs on your journey through this imaginative landscape. Here, the small violin from Sherlock's home, there, the pile of seashells collected over the years, holding echoes of pirate adventures. The fat teal goblets (crafted from clay and love by another sister) on the top shelf, a promise of abundance, and a cup always filled to the brim with stories and copper pennies.

Here is a secret map of the stories you will pen. The slim volume that slips from two hardbacks pressed together? Yours. You will watch these new stories appear from your perch at your writing desk, spinning new beginnings from the layers of old books.

La Llorona

She came for you once.

You weren't more than seven or eight. The marvel of the story was not in the bony handprint left on your windowpane, but in the fact that you were able to push her away – terrified as you were. Even then, you could access the strength written into your blood.

You knew of no version of her tale that spoke of survivors. Like the insides of a penny dreadful, there were only accounts of willful children devoured by this lonesome creature in her perpetual, unfruitful search for redemption. It was all broken hearts and bitterness gone to seed. La Llorona, victim of her own pride and shame, drowning her sorrows in rage as she drowned her children, her own half-formed life. It was the Rio Grande you must be careful of, you had learned, for that is where she roams, feet sinking into the muddy banks, the moon illuminating black hair plastered to her face and casting her white dress into shadow.

But that night you learned any body of water could hold her.

It was one of those cold, wild nights in October when the wind was unruly, violently throwing dead leaves against your house. The air was full of the scent of burning cedar from nearby chimneys. The day had been full of too many ghost stories at school, greedily gobbled up on the playground. You knew you would pay for the cheap thrills later, like stuffing yourself with sweets that would eventually turn your stomach against you. It was so much easier to speak of ghosts and monsters in the daylight. But when the shadows lengthened across your backyard and you no longer basked in the safety of your autumnal sun, you knew there was more to these stories than just words to pass the time between math and reading. The weight in your belly was proof enough. And when sleep found you, it was as wild and restless as the night, filled with the playground gossip of the Weeping Woman.

That was how La Llorona found you. It was as if your thoughts called her to you, drawing her attention away from the river. You thought it was the wind howling at first. You had woken with a start, foisted out of nightmares to wailing just outside your home. Then it was the scratching at the window. *Must be your neighbor's pine tree reaching its thick branches across the dividing wall and scraping against your panes,* you told yourself. *It is only nature running its course.*

But then you began to think of that neighbor and the swimming pool in his backyard. You thought of the child that was taken into its depths, never to come back. You had seen the child at the bottom of that pool once, felt the tug on your heel as you tried to break the surface. You had never met him before the water took him but knew with clarity when you broke free from his grasp that he had never left that pool. He was milky eyes and water ripples now. It was then you knew you could never cross that wall again – the same wall a dark pine tree reached across to knock against the solid brick of your home.

Perhaps it was La Llorona who took the child and keeps him there still. With that thought, the howling wind became her cries; the branches at your window, her fingernails trying to claw her way in. Coming, coming for you. You vowed never to listen to the ghost stories on the playground ever again – a short-lived promise – and you vowed never to let yourself become like the child still at the bottom of the pool. That one you kept. Within the safety of your bed, chin-deep in covers, you realized that however you might have summoned her – curiosity, candy, a shared name? – you had the power to send her away. You had to – *must* – believe in the blood wisdom coursing through your veins.

So you closed your eyes and focused. You felt your home around you. The solidity of the brick and the warmth and the love and the security. You pushed away thoughts of weeping women and drowned children, and replaced them with images of the faded pattern on your blanket, the scent of dinner lingering in the air. Tortillas warm from the skillet. Green chile stew and pinto beans. Laughter. Homework. The clinking of dishes being washed and the *brush brush* of the broom across kitchen floor during cleanup. And love. So much love.

The violent howling outside was no match for it. It – she – could not get in. She didn't understand what that emotion was, had never tasted it, and so it left her disoriented, lost, in search of the river's familiar grounds. Slowly, the wind died. The scratching at your window stopped, and you drifted off to sleep. It wasn't until years later that you understood what had really happened. It was your home that protected you and protects you still, that ephemeral thing made up of bricks and memories and the thoughts you choose to entertain. Now older, maybe even wiser – but still no less susceptible to the thrills of a good ghost story – you carry your home with you, protection against any force that would pull you under ...

... Because she never stopped trying. She came for you once again when you were much, much older. She didn't like what she couldn't claim. You were another unfinished story she couldn't get her hands on. So she waited and she watched. Eventually, she used an ancestral blood clot to find you, crawled through an open window and watched as you slept.

It was her wet hair dripping onto your face that woke you. She wanted you conscious for this. Wanted you to know that she had found her home in a well of bitterness that she felt would suit you nicely.

But you were so much stronger than the little girl only half-aware of her full potential. This time, you flung your covers back rather than retreat behind them. You closed your eyes. And piece by piece, you forgot her. The cold droplets she tattooed on your face. Her wet black hair. Then her white dress. Her empty eyes went next. Then the bitterness. Then the pride. Then the grief. The last was the hardest to let go of. You condemned her to the salted water of her tears. May she drown in them, for she has no place in your home. In your heart. You, too, had been waiting for this moment. Once and for all, you banished her to the muddy underworld of her own making. You sealed that clot with burning sage and crystal-clear intentions to live in the now.

The howling outside your door was just wind. The tears, just rain. The scratching at your door, just knobby branches tasting bricks.

You got up and closed the window. Crawled back in bed. And slept soundly.

On Bravery

I am learning to be brave.

Ask me to bend like the supple flesh of an aspen tree and I will. I will sway and dip in time to your blustery demands. Watch me weave together a life out of nothing but stray thread from my coat pocket and a handful of experiences. Know that I can let the candle burn all night and do what needs to be done. I have made my peace with beeswax in my hair and ink under my fingernails.

But ask me to let go of those things – those carefully crafted versions of myself – and I don't know. My heart stops. How can I plant a small seed in soil that I'm not sure is fertile enough?

You see, I am learning to be brave.

Learning to know that the seed, a small husk holding only a possibility, is as strong and hearty as the aspen it will become. It is only a fragile flicker of promise now, but watch it grow when I feed it dreams. Trust the soil. Trust the seed. Trust my hands holding the earth. Then what? What will I do when the silvery bark that holds me together is like so many bits of chain mail around my heart, not the tender skin it once was? Let it be a breathing, living force again. Not a fossil.

But to do that, I must learn to be brave. Reach beyond the comfort of my ink-stained skin, and let the tree sap flow through my roots and hair. Let the chain mail become silver vines that hug and ground and fall across my back like so many wishes. And when my heart, free from those metal bindings, feels like a fresh bruise or an open wound, I will enjoy the way it pulses and ferociously mends itself with a compress of heartbreak, blood, and dirt.

Watch as the soil loosens around me to make room for new homes, for new seeds. Watch as I forget to hold on to every leaf and let them fade, fall, and bloom just as they should.

Grounding and Gardening

It is a relief to find the weekend upon you, two whole days of gardening stretched out before you. The week had been one of transformation, skin shedding, disorientation. You need roots and stems to remind you that your home is in the possibility of a hollowed-out seed husk.

You take comfort in the way the dirt feels between your fingers as you cast aside the little spade in favor of pushing loose soil around with your hands. The color of coffee beans, the earth smells of wet minerals and growing things. Even the little salt crystals that you stir into the soil ground you in the here and now. They purify your mind, absorb any darkness, and transform it into nourishment for the seeds you then bury. Round radish kernels and thin little lettuce pips are soothing reminders that, one pod at a time, you conjure new life firmly rooted in the present.

The sharp scent of rosemary already welcomes good energies into your home, while the light perfume of lemon balm promises future healing tonics. You dig your hands deeper into the soil and gently tuck your oregano into its planter, making sure to surround it with plenty of life-giving dirt. Already you are thinking of the Sunday night pasta made more delicious because of this herb, or the Friday night pizza given an extra zip after you return from your patio garden with cuttings from this zesty herb.

With each plant that you settle into the safety of your pots, you feel more firmly grounded, gently cradled by the loving embrace of the earth. The week's events that made you feel disoriented, untethered from this world, have lost their sting. In their place is only the quiet industry of gardening, the soft breeze tickling the trees beyond your patio, and the mellow chatter of finches. You look forward to the harvest of dark rose cherry tomatoes and

Armenian cucumbers, even as you remind yourself to buy carrot seeds because a tomato plant is nothing without a ring of carrots to keep it company. Those two, they can never be apart for long.

Later, when all your plants are potted, and you linger over a glass of fresh lemonade on your patio admiring the cheerful basil and wild mint getting accustomed to their new home, you realize how for two blissful days, you have not thought of the past, old ghosts, or what-might-have-beens. Those you gave to your compost – you can image the worms wriggling their way through half-dead dreams or the thick scales of a past self. Their burial ground will become such lush soil for new beginnings. You simply tended to your potted garden. It is so obvious now. These plants, this careful act of tending living things, are what you're about. One small seed at a time, you lay the groundwork for present enjoyment and future harvest.

Letting Go of Past Lives

I have been all of three women. A Belle. A Book. And a Candle. That is what they used to bind me, to keep me from myself.

The Belle went first. She learned early on that there was more to the world than swanning and preening and letting her peals of laughter ring like a breeze through chimes. Surface things only took a debutant so far. Barely just outside her doorstep, in fact. And she grew tired of powdering her face until it looked whiter than it was. *Spanish* was the desired nomenclature for her bronze skin. Or in another circle entirely, rouging her cheeks so that she might look duskier. Beauty was in the eye of the beholder, after all, but what if she had grown tired of hungry gazes? So she put away her laces and stopped batting her lashes. Still, traces of her can be found in the unnecessary frills on dresses, and the way I pine – no, that's not the right word – *hope* there is someone to share this world with when the moon is full and the night seems to stretch on forever.

Then there was the Book. She was all corners and ruffled pages. She couldn't handle surface either, so she roughed hers with pulpy matter and pen scratchings. She wrapped her skeleton in thick leather and bound her spine with glue, needle, and thread. What a story she'd become! She let the ink seep into her blood and her eyes fill with narratives. Her hair was a nest of plot threads and her heart, one giant happily ever after. But a woman couldn't survive on stories alone, no matter how romantic the notion. And when she could no longer tell the difference between her paper princes and the people around her, she knew she needed to be more than page and pen.

That was when I became the Candle. Burned away each page and gently singed her sharp corners so that they were soft and rounded. She burned and burned, and then committed those ashes of that other woman to the ground. She was golden in her beeswax skin, warm to the touch. But hungry, always hungry. Eager to lick anything with her fat flame. Ever in need of just one more absolution.

Traces of these women can still be found in the corners of my mind and in the puckered scars along my body where the Candle got greedy and seared new skin after eating up all those dusty chapters. Or in the way I still find ink smudges on the inside of my arm, though I know I've scrubbed my body clean. It's not so easy to bury the dead. Even when I've said goodbye, there's still the beeswax scab I pluck from my knee and my indefatigable desire to dance, though I suppose that last one's worth keeping.

I am no longer the Candle, either. The decision was purely practical. I cannot burn and burn and burn and still hope to taste this world in slow, delicate sips. Yet I struggle to know what or who is next. I now know them for what they are – the Belle, the Book, and the Candle. They are the tools I used to bind me, to keep me from myself. They are memories floating in my blood, memories of a time when women like me needed to be bound. I am only just learning, as I pull a stray book-thread from my spine, that no one can bind me unless I let them. And even bound, I am never tamed. Just resting. Better, though, to give myself the freedom they cannot stand to see. Freedom that I am not always comfortable having.

I am molting – shedding – and yet, for the first time, I do not know what I am becoming. Now that I am looking, I find traces of these past lives everywhere: a nest of my glossy hair in the tree outside my window, a few pulpy scales sitting in my bathtub where I first began to shed around my ear. There is even an ink-stained fingernail at the bottom of my coin jar. I am almost afraid to look under my bed. Who knows what I might find there. Certainly more than dust bunnies and moving boxes. Perhaps I might find more perfume-stained specters like the one I now see in my closet, staring back at me between penny loafers and Peter Pan collared dresses. And here I thought I took no baggage with me.

I cannot stand my home. I am choked by the memories of what I no longer want to be. I run outside. Fall on my knees in the wet earth. Feel the weight of my body sinking into rich dirt. Relish the release of three women I'd rather not see – be – again.

Then I find myself in the smell of things growing. Not a Belle. Not a Book. Not a Candle at all, but a seed. I'm a seed.

I am a Seed.

And I let my first tentative green tendril spill from my husk and curl toward the sky.

The Apple

The original forbidden fruit. At home with Eve and wicked queens, Aphrodite and writers looking to sink their teeth into something more than fleshy prose. It is the promise of knowledge, desires slaked, immortality, and a full belly. Blamed for original sins and poisoned thoughts. In reality, it's only the messenger of whoever holds it and worms her thoughts into its core. That is to say nothing of the seeds. Toxic if you swallow too many at once, yet bearing the future in their thick brown shells. You mustn't be greedy and force an orchard to bloom within you, only savor the fruit it offers. Still, you understand the desire to harvest it all for yourself. The apple is a potent container for unblemished potential.

And yet so unassuming.

What is it about this small misshapen fruit, like the one perched lopsidedly on a stack of books at your desk, that makes the world run mad after it? Certainly not its appearance. It never does look like the storybook picture of a red jewel awaiting only the presence of your lips upon its flesh to make it complete. It is streaked with gold and rose stripes, a thick nub sticking out of its top. The apple fits neatly in the palm of your hand so that your thumb can tickle the fuzz protruding from its bottom. It smells of ripened leaves and the slow setting of the sun. At last, you sink your teeth into it. The taste of honeysuckle flesh and skin like plant vines floods your mouth. It is sweet, yes, and pleasant to bite into, with the satisfying crunch and smack of the lips as you make your way to its core.

But even now, as you stare at its hourglass form, its full body a faint memory of teeth marks along its edges, you wonder at its ability to tempt us, to seduce us into grasping for things beyond our private Edens. And wonder still if it is wise to submit to that temptation. To look beyond this oasis of books and words and a delicious view of a tree in its autumnal glory outside your window. With this rumination, you find you are only half-satisfied with your snack, as if the taste of its flesh generates more hunger than it slakes. You want more. More of *what*, you couldn't say. There is simply a sense of longing blooming in your stomach and radiating outwards through your limbs for something you have yet to experience. So new is this feeling, so deep this longing that it has no name or form, just a promise of the unknown manifesting itself in a small apple core whose seeds peek out of its center.

You realize it then, what power the apple holds: Wonder. The ability to make us want and wonder and dream beyond our own havens, to taste a little bit of life just outside our doorstep. With that in mind, you finish your writing for the day. The words have satisfied you as much as the apple. Enough to whet your appetite. Now you go to feast upon experience.

On Gratitude

Here is something no heavier than a feather, no larger than the minuscule crack in an acorn's shell through which new life can seep. You find it nestled in a mound of the season's first baby artichokes at the market or buried in the tissue paper wrapping of a gift from someone who knows you love to watch things blossom. It's even at the bottom of a wine glass after a long day.

It offers only a memory of loving hands stitching two frayed ends back together where there once was just a hole in your coat pocket. It produces nothing but a soft sigh as you settle into your favorite reading chair to savor the company of your books. And where others debate over the fullness of a glass, you see only that you have a cup the color of the sky on a clear day capable of holding anything. One of your mother's making. You always think of her hands over wet clay when you drink from it. She was the one who taught you the power of a handful of dirt. No, *soil*.

And when two small hands latch on to your fat thumb, you feel only a swelling chest and a reminder that you are more than just books and paperwork. You have hands and a heart, though you sometimes forget. The sunrise is there to reinforce this ... this ... *aliveness*, asking you only to pause and enjoy a sky streaked with lilac and gold before the day is fully awake.

You see everywhere, signs of abundance rather than absence, wings rather than cages. And finally, enjoyment in the way your feet always take you back to your doorstep and the pleasure, deep and full like your first breath of the day, in knowing you are home.

The Hunt for a New Read

But the last one was so good.

If only it was longer or you hadn't turned through the pages so fast, greedily gobbling up the words like a child stuffing her mouth with sweets. It wasn't your fault, you rationalize. How could you not keep reading? How could you not dip back into that world every chance you got, losing yourself in the absinth and fog, the plot and the twists? It would be like asking a starving soul to forgo the marvels that sustain it. The book needed to be longer, was all; or somehow have more pages to it so that you could linger in its inky embrace.

But these ruminations are just that, remnants of a story you've already devoured. They won't solve your problem. Only a new adventure will. How else can you best untangle the plot of your own life or make sense of the moments where it seems to fold back on itself, replaying a chapter you've long since passed? You know of no other way to understand that this or that upheaval is merely pushing you forward along the pages of your life, so that you don't get too comfortable at the bottom of a paragraph! You shout out this plea, though you don't know to whom. The books themselves, maybe? Or the ink on the pages? Both remain silent. But you know there is no other compass as reliable as a good story.

Perhaps you will try this book here. It's been sitting on your shelf a while. You flip through the worn but new-to-you pages from a paperback, half-ready to fall in love at the first sentence. But no. The heroine is not so likable (when did harsh become the new virtuous?), the streets not so intriguing (the descriptions as heavy as the brick holding the buildings together). Maybe if you gave it a few more pages, but why should you? You shouldn't have to work that hard. Shouldn't feel that each page is made of lead and so, so difficult to turn. You cast that dead end aside as you do a number of others. One because it does not quite capture the essence of the clatter of hooves on cobblestone the way the last one did, another because the front illustration was not imaginative enough. Sometimes the covers do tell the truth, as you found when you tried to sink beneath its surface. This one is too serious. That one a light confection of silliness. Where is that perfect blend of wit and gravitas?

It is a battle within yourself, searching for a new place to plant your imagination and watch it bloom. Yet you are loath to leave your old haunt. Eventually, you abandon the bookshelf altogether, throwing yourself at the mercy of eBook samples. Surely there must be *something* to sink your mind into. But the same old dilemma greets you in your cyber realm. This book is too slow, that one too fast, falling over itself in its hurry to get through the plot. The tone there is too thin for such a substantial topic like a solemn cream puff, leaving you feeling strangely like a grave breeze. Yet this next one is too heavy, weighted down by verbose prose and self-importance – hardly the stuff of guilty pleasures. You begin to feel that you must write yourself what you best want to read. But that will take time; while you are infinitely patient as you tend the plant that will bear your future fruit, you likewise recognize that you are a woman of immediate gratification. You need new fuel now, the better to sustain your writing practice.

You sift and sift, revisiting old books and searching for new ones, until it happens. You stumble upon a gem in the pile of simply-will-not-do books. It's the cover that draws you in first. The hint of adventure, and yes, the flash of skin, then the back description: danger, daring, set against a Gothic backdrop. Your favorite. You cannot conceive how you missed this book or discarded it minutes earlier. It makes perfect sense, seeming to mold itself to your needs. Now that you look at it, you can't even remember where you bought it or how long it has been sitting on your shelf. Regardless, you are grateful that it exists, that it is in your hands now. Your fingers slip between the covers and find that perfect spot. The one that makes you giggle, or shiver, or wonder, begging you to turn the page. Without realizing it, you have found a cozy nook amidst the pile of books. You curl up there and disappear into your new read.

You remember now why you bought the book in the first place. You can hardly understand why you haven't read it sooner as the immediacy of the last read fades in the unfolding of the new one.

On Hollyhocks

They are your wild desert flowers with no self-control. They don't need it, for it doesn't do their petals any good. Only the breeze and the sun and the expansive turquoise sky do. They fill their open faces with light they collect and send it snaking down their roots. There, they can store it in their plot of earth, held in place only by the thin, strong threads of life that gather dirt and minerals and water around themselves in a protective nest. That is hollyhocks below. The roots and stems allow them to stretch to the sky and fearlessly blossom into fat, joyful flowers, one on top of the other in a noisy cluster.

They are not your coy primroses nor your restless impatiens (sounding too much like *impatience*) that bloom time and time again. Sometimes on your writing desk, sometimes in your garden, already eager to start the cycle once more even as they have not yet made it through their first bloom. They don't care about covering the ground, as does your flowering thyme, which is more than happy to crawl across the earth in a slow bid for more territory. Nor do they need to make a point of their beauty like the rose, always looking to be the object of everyone's affection.

No, these hollyhocks simply *are.*

They are happy in themselves, firmly planted in their nourishing nest of roots, water, and soil. These brassy flowers want light around them, growing strong in the heat of the desert, thriving on the kisses of bees and the caresses of dry air. They stretch tall to touch the sky, gifting it with their jewel-toned petals of pink, purple, red. They return the bees' love by offering up their fat stamen coated in pollen. *Eat,* they tell the bees. *Eat.* Even when their flowers fade, they still hold strong. It is as if they cannot contain themselves, wantonly spreading their thick black seeds everywhere, letting them spill over flagstone and dirt, peppering flower beds and getting carried away in the wind to find new homes, new nests. They cannot help but multiply.

Even when their hulls have dried out and their flowers have faded, they pepper the earth with their thick seeds. You want them for yourself, these puckered, withered husks whose insides are lined with life-affirming disks. You fill your pockets with them. You let them spill across your garden path. Let the wind sweep them away. Let the ground take them into its loving embrace. Soon there will be more blossoms. More flowers reaching to the sky.

They are living proof that lush life can bloom – *thrive* – in any desert.

Why I Won't Wait on the Sidelines to Dance

Because I don't need permission to dance. Especially not when it comes to feeling the heat of salsa sabrosa in my bones or the slow, coy bounce of bachata in my hips. I will not waste precious time sitting on the sidelines waiting to be asked to the floor like some forlorn teenage girl at prom – not when I can be a song beating out the rhythm of my joy. I will merely extend my hand and see who takes it. And if there aren't enough partners, I will make the music my companion, letting its congas and bass wrap around me as I sway and dip and turn.

I have allowed myself to sit too long on these foldout chairs, a would-be wallflower wilting under the silence, the invisibility of my hesitation. My indecision and doubt are deafening, drowning out the blast of horns and *boom boom* of the bongo. *It is no longer enough*, a small voice inside me whispers, *to sit and observe*. It is then, when I admit this to myself, that the music grows louder, drowning out the doubt in my pulse. Abstaining from the pleasure right in front of me is no virtue.

And it is a pleasure. A pleasure to never be without a dance partner because they see I am unafraid of hips and hands and feet and sweat. It is a pleasure to twirl around the dance floor, allowing each turn to peel away one more petal from that old wallflower until I am the boldest expression of my dance.

I am no longer vulnerable when that last petal falls to the ground, naked as I am, because I have forever banished those years of sideline-sitting. In my desire to move my body, there is freedom. There is power in my grace, though it is my job to follow. For while I may lose a step or fall out of rhythm, I am on the dance floor all the same. There is joy in learning a new language of heartbeat, footsteps, and cowbell.

And I will stay on that dance floor, those old foldout chairs a distant memory of some other woman.

Let Me Be

Let me be the river forever creating ripples in the stillness, still in its eternal movement through its clay path. Let me be the wind that whispers of lives past, hopes not yet lived, as my stormy fingers twine around the earth's wild curls, or let me be the heartbeat between breaths.

Let me be the memory of seeds resting in my bones, the code buried in the hollyhocks' chunky black discs stacked along my spine. Just let me be the quiet of a morning before it is kissed by the sun or touched by birdsong. I ask for nothing else. Only this promise to free me from the confines of others' expectations – or worse, my own – and the sting of turning away from stories I don't own, shouldn't inhabit. Give me the freedom of my own exhale, without pressure to inhale burdens that are not mine. I am the songbird, not the nest where cuckoos bury their eggs.

Let me be the clean slate, the open swath of unblemished potential spread out before you like a field of grain not yet harvested, or the desert monsoon, still unknowing if it will rain down upon this earth or let the ripe clouds sail beyond the horizon. Let me be the dream conjured out of lunar light, shining through the crystals on your nightstand …

… And that precarious universe between sleep and wakefulness. Let me be. Just let me be.

Dancing in the Rain

Last night I danced in the rain.

I sang with the wind. I spread my hands high over my head and tried to touch the dark clouds weighing down the evening sky. I called upon that storm to sweep away the cobwebs from my mind, to let the plump raindrops fall upon my upturned face, a soothing balm across the tender center between both eyes.

I let the distant rumble of thunder echo in my bones and the promise of lightning tickle my long wet hair. I did this, making myself one with the rhythm of nature, allowing myself to understand the bigness of it, the fullness of this universe that goes beyond myself and within myself. My bare feet rooted themselves in puddles as I twirled among the raindrops and clouds and air thick with cleansing desert magic. There is no room for dust in my heart in this moment of abundance.

I was a spirit dancing among other spirits: trees, grass, mountains, and their guardians. I was a raindrop covering the earth with my love. I was the quiet in the storm, the stillness in the dance, the held breath between one clap of thunder and another. I was the whisper of the earth's smile.

On Sunbathing

In this moment, you are like a turtle perched on a log, unwilling to move an inch for fear the sun will not fully coat you in its delicious honeyed kiss. You want every bit of light to cover you, soak into your skin, and fill your body with the heat of your desert sky. It is pure nourishment, your soul forged anew under that solar gaze. It is as if there are tiny cleansing flames licking your skin, leaving nothing but liquid amber in their wake. The world softens as you linger in its warm embrace, opening you up to hazy daydreams among the drone of bees and quiet chatter of birds.

You would take all your clothes off if you could. You think wistfully once again of the joy in secluded nooks and private gardens. Let yourself wear nothing but sunlight until your skin returns to its natural bronze color, faded after a winter buried under too many layers of clothes. But you can forget all those layers now under the sun's caress. The tender pale flesh you expose to its heat begins to ripen, the last of the frost melting from your ribs and collarbone until there is only a small puddle of lukewarm water beneath your perch. It will be nothing but a faint watermark within a few minutes, a memory of snowfall and cedar-burning fireplaces. You don't need to gaze directly into the light to know the influence it has over you, the way it makes you open up to a world of delicious possibilities. They speak of rose-colored glasses, but for you, it is golden-hued spectacles revealing a world drenched in amber purity, each moment of beauty crystalized in its gaze.

You want to map the sun's passage as it makes its way along your body, tattooing your limbs with its essence. It starts with your closed eyelids, its touch surprisingly gentle across your lashes, then winds its way down to your toes and through your fingertips, luxuriating in the whole length of you. Forget being the turtle. The longer you bathe in this light, you feel yourself to be a morning glory, unfurling her vines so that they wrap around the spiral of the sun, her bloom readily opening outwards under the tender pressure of the day's heat. Even your hair shines with the radiance of this luminous touch, softening into a honey-red, after months of being the color of dark earth. You are powerful under its gaze, a body of golden light and infinite possibility.

Even when it makes way for the moon, you still feel its fire within you. More than a morning glory, you must be a salamander to be able to store the heat of the sun in your body, although it has left the sky and the earth has cooled with the inevitable darkness. Your skin is still warm, and your insides glow from a day spent daydreaming, drifting, losing track of everything except the way the sunlight burns away impurities. You are left with nothing but your truest essence, hot to the touch, eternally fueled by light created by your time in the sun.

The Dandelion

A weed.

The bane of the perfect lawn's existence, flinging its seeds wherever the wind will take them. Eternal survivor. Oblivious to weed killer, lawn mower, calloused hands attempting to uproot it from concrete cracks. Never as beloved as the luscious rose or the frail beauty of the orchid, yet worthy of its own song. No love ballad but a bittersweet strain of healing and grounding. So kick it about. Pull at it. Neglect it. Grab fistfuls of its fluff and try to keep them from escaping your curled-up fist. You can't stop its medicine.

Under the right touch, you cultivate it. The hands that would rip this flower from the ground, happy to banish it from her plot of earth, instead tenderly collect leaves, stems, roots, flowers to add to her home apothecary. She knows the sunflower's bastard cousin is the floral embodiment of the celestial bodies that rule her. Its golden flower, the sun in petal form, the white head emerging as that sun fades, your moon; the constellation of seeds needing only a windy kiss to send them scattering across the earth, her stars. How many flowery universes does it nestle in its head? That is a conversation best left to lazy afternoons sprawled in the grass at home among the lion-toothed leaves growing over green blades. A conversation best had through whispered wishes.

For this gardener knows the potent magic of the dandelion, detoxifying the seat of the soul. It is a joy to feel the weed flushing out stagnation and poison from the body, rooting her spirit once again to the earth. She steeps her treasure in hot water and drinks the healing potion, reveling in how the dandelion spreads through her body like its seeds spread through the city, finding each forgotten nook, each empty corner and filling it up with its light.

Once inside the body, it makes its way through the liver and up to that soft space between her eyes. With this gift of sight, she can see that much of life takes place beyond the veil, as the dandelion begins its life as a possibility buried in darkness. Past, present, future swirl at the bottom of her cup of weed tea. If she won't take tea, she might divine her fortune by plucking the petals off its yellow head until she sees the answer inscribed on the last remaining strand of light. Or she could return to that afternoon in the grass and blow upon its frothy white head to make a wish, to cast a dream into the wind, and know that one day it will come back to her.

And yet, this healing collection of seeds, roots, and leaves is labeled as nothing more exciting than a weed. Only revealing its magic to those who are prepared to see past the limited glory of its finer-looking cousins, only sharing its bounty with those ready to be healed and willing to leave it a few concrete cracks in which it can thrive.

On Red Chile Stew

Your home in a bowl. The most profound medicine stored in the waxy dried pods of your desert fruit. A cure-all that warms your bones and mends your heart, more chicken noodle soup than chicken noodle soup. As with any remedy, the healing is in the making as much as it is in the dosage.

You grind your red chile pods, already softened from a long soak in warm water, and run them through a sieve until you are left with nothing but a velvety red liquid to fill your soul as it fills your bowl. To that, you add a cup full of memories. Your family kitchen filled with the scent of cooking pinto beans. The taste of good New Mexican beer and lively conversation on your tongue. The counter and your apron coated in flour from rolling out fresh tortillas. Even the smart of heat on your thumb and index finger as you flip those tortillas over on the hot skillet. After the memories come the pork sizzling in the pot, then the sprinkling of good intentions, and the garlic your mother always reminds you to put in. Stock is next, poured over the pork in time to Bebel Gilberto crooning in the background, and the promise of a nourishing life. Last is the pureed chile itself, the final ingredient that turns the soup base into an alchemical epiphany.

Now you can only wait and let time do its job. As with life, so with stew. That last thought, perhaps it was the tequila talking. You turn to your tortillas, neatly stacked inside a cotton kitchen towel embroidered with cornflower-blue blossoms. A pot of pinto beans simmers on the stove, just as it would in your childhood home. Some things don't change. You wash the dishes piled in the sink, a chore as integral to your chile recipe as that final dash of sea salt into the pot of pintos.

On to the dosage. A by-the-book prescription would call for two parts chile stew and one part beans, ladled into one of your mother's mica bowls, taken with a whole wheat tortilla slathered in ghee and washed down with a cold microbrew. Repeat as needed. A potent cure, to be sure. But you know the best way to take your medicine, an old family secret: straight from the pot.

Still in your flour-coated apron – you always were messy in the kitchen – and bare feet, you filch a tortilla from your still-hot stack and stand over your stove. The steam from the bubbling stew washes over your face, coating it in the soothing perfume of a New Mexican home. You tear your tortilla into fourths and dip one of the triangles into the ruby liquid before making sure to scoop up some of the pork. You take one bite, then another. The spiciness hits your tongue first, then the earthy sweetness of the chiles. And right behind that, the bright flood of warmth hitting your chest and radiating outwards. A sign your medicine is working.

Living Your Creed

You want the world to be the inside of a seed, its possibility coded in each wrinkle and groove and in a perpetual state of becoming. Better put: You want it so that the grass is not just green but that indescribable shade of a summer afternoon, and so that the ladybug crawling across your fingers is a polka-dotted message from the universe, not a wind-blown beetle.

That is your dream at the bottom of a well only you know how to find. That is the voice you want to coax from the cracks in the cement like a dandelion thriving in its makeshift home. What do you want to create in this wild, unruly world? How can you possibly explain to the whispering trees that you must live deliciously?

If you know each seed you plant will blossom, you must sow wisely. If you know each thought is a thread coloring the tapestry of your life, you must think carefully. If you know that your lungs need fresh air and open space to fill them up, you must find a land without fences in which to breathe deeply and preserve that space.

And if you know that only you can create your future, you must wake every morning ready to carve out the next curve in your path. When you learn your life is made up of conversations with the universe, you must speak with the universe often, shout out to it, sing to it, and listen to its response even if no one else can understand or hear the exchange. They see only dust, where you see stars.

I Used to Write on Napkins

Beside me sits a wrinkled napkin, a yellow-brown ring half-formed around its center; the offending teacup sits just beside it now. I cannot say why it caught my eye as I load up the papers I've been grading, getting ready for the next item on my to-do list – only that it stirs something inside me, loosens an almost forgotten fact from the crevices of my mind:

I used to write on napkins.

Even used-up ones like these. Just out of braces and feeling Oh-So-Adult with my new teeth and my after-school hostess job, I decided I had stories in me. Big stories. Important stories. Deep stories … about … who knew what. But when to write? An even bigger question than *what* to write. I figured that would answer itself, so long as I could convince the ever-moving clock that words were worth my time. Reading was no issue, I did that everywhere and at all times. In bed. During long car rides. Splayed out on the grass when the weather was nice and curled up in my golden reading nook when it wasn't. During class, sneaking my book under my desk while the teacher lectured. In the bathroom. Before dinner and after dinner. And whenever I could squeeze in a page between chores and class periods.

But I wasn't just a reader anymore. I was a Writer. And that came with responsibilities. Like finding time to write.

I was still under the vague impression that writers – Real Writers – must devote every moment of the clock hands, spinning around its face, to build stories out of ink and fantasy. But I was a high school student, an identity I only grudgingly admitted to, and a pub hostess (perhaps, I hoped, I looked more worldly than my seventeen years). And I lacked the funds to run away to Paris to write – another thing I learned Real Writers did. So I squeezed it in after cleaning tables and seating customers, in those brief stretches between filling water glasses and folding napkins ...

... Those napkins again.

I kept the cloth ones for the customers and contented myself with cheap cocktail napkins to scribble on. Those thin four-by-four squares seemed like they soaked up the most interesting tales anyway. On one frayed edge was the start of my first novel (mercifully gone now), on a crumpled corner, a nonsensical ditty. On the inside flap of another napkin, the quick sketch of pub scenes: the couple getting too cozy at a corner table, the boisterous bar-side conversation of half-drunk friends, the bartender taking it all in, unflappable.

I would stuff these worldly scraps into my pocket, as someone would crumpled tissues, and pull them out when I got home smelling of fries and cleaning solution. I had more food stains on my shirt and pants than ink on my fingers. My feet would hurt from running around all night, and I could barely keep my eyes open. I wanted a shower. And pajamas. And maybe some of those fries sitting in the leftovers box in the fridge. But I was sure to remember to rescue my words. Carefully, I would untangle them and stack them upon my writing desk to cure overnight. These were my future, after all. Perhaps tomorrow, they would yield the seeds of a story.

So I wrote that first novel on napkins, and later buried it in my mother's compost, and much of my second one, so much better than the last – but also left for worm food. I'd educated myself within the confines of the napkin's one-inch, ridged border about characters and settings and plots and what was worth recording. I'd flourished in the cheap paper's soft center, daring to push my words beyond the thin limits set by others ... because it was just a napkin. A flimsy little thing scratched up by a ballpoint pen that I could ball up and stuff in my pocket.

Now, staring at the stack of graded essays and that stained napkin, I wondered where that fearlessness had gone. Where the determination to write and write and write had gone, once I'd allowed myself to call myself a Writer and graduated from napkins to a laptop. Things were no different now. True, I'd traded cleaning tables of their dirty dishes for cleaning up prose, the student's desk for the teacher's office. But there were still pockets of time, pockets begging to have napkins stuffed in them. Still stories to tell, though who knows if they are good or deep or whatever I had once hoped for them.

I eye my watch – those hands winding around heavy numbers – and glance back at my napkin. The best stories begin on the fringes, then find their home in the middle and back around again to the corners. I still have a few minutes before I really need to go. So I settle in, however briefly. I take up that napkin and a pen – and I write.

On Autumn Sweaters

Last night, you found yourself rummaging through your closet, looking for that one colorless, shapeless sweater you've had for years and years. The one you can't remember where you got it from, but somehow always turn to when the nights get longer and cooler. The soft cotton on the inside has been loved off by time and use, so all that remains is a thin pelt. The sleeves are frayed and overstretched, the neck a loose ribbon around your shoulders. There it is, buried in the back with your coats. It occurs to you as you pull this soft shell over your head that it is officially sweater season, and that you have one for just about every important occasion. This is the sweater you wear at the end of the week when all you want to do is curl up on the couch, eat popcorn, and watch a movie.

But there are so many others that you love and look forward to wearing as the earth prepares itself for a season of quiet and rest. There is the basic oatmeal sweater, perfect for rolling up its sleeves for a morning in the kitchen baking bread or dipping apples in warm caramel and nuts. It is homey and solid, like the loaf you just pulled from the oven. And you can't forget the rose-hued one that falls off your shoulders, ideal for an afternoon of drinking cinnamon tea and getting lost (found?) in a book of fairy tales, mysteries, Gothic novels ... doesn't matter. But the sweater does, somehow making the afternoon complete, allowing you to settle down, doze off in your overstuffed chair, the rose cloth wrapped around you like a blanket.

Or there is the heather purple one essential for raking up leaves and putting your garden to rest for the season. It is light enough to keep you cool as you labor, with long sleeves to protect you from the prickly bones of dried plants, the skeletal trees, and the early morning bite. You don't fret over messing it up as you would one of your teaching blouses because it was made for getting dirt and crumbled leaves on its cuffs.

You look at the sweater you are wearing now, the one you paused your writing for long enough to slide your arms into before returning to that next page. The open window brings in the cool, lush air of the season. Your writing cardigan, a sub-genre of the autumn sweater, and cup of chai, echoing the heavy scents of autumn, chase away the chill. You love this sweater perhaps most of all. Though you say that about each one as you don it and feel the memories stitched into its fabric rubbing against your skin. This sweater is long and faded, the color of sage, with oversized pockets for storing seeds or tea leaves or a few words. There are no buttons to this cardigan, so you must make peace with the fact that it must always be open, as you must be to your stories and experiences, wherever they may take you. This one is made for loosely wrapping around yourself, just as you wrap your words around you for comfort and healing as you descend into the realm of stories.

Yes, it is sweater season now. You look forward to being once again in the folds of these unassuming garments that reflect the quietest, most intimate snapshots of your life. The moments you live without ceremony, or the awareness of anything other than dipping your caramel apple into a shallow tray of sunflower seeds.

Playing with Herbs

You have your jars of herbs lined up before you like wild soldiers. Blue jars and green jars and clear jars with logos like puckered scars across their smooth faces. Each is stuffed with gifts from the ground – fat golden flowers and thick roots and long needles – each its own medicine. Here is calendula, that happy marigold, ready to soothe irritated skin and frayed minds. There is ginger root, the fiery cleanser of the solar plexus, stoking the heat, the determination within yourself. Tucked in the back is that brash kitchen herb rosemary, a fearless, sharp evergreen that clears the mind and heals your tired bones.

You let the scents of each open jar mingle and cloud your nose as you take first a pinch of this herb and then a scoop of that. You want something; your body is humming, calling for the soothing wisdom of these plants. They answer your call with the gentle melody of tiny buds bouncing against the sides of your small marble mixing bowl, dried leaves whooshing into the pile of your new blend.

You inhale the rich, grassy scent of alfalfa leaves, hungry for their nourishment. You search through your jars, looking for alfalfa's mate, that balancing force that tempers the mouthful of mowed grass with sweet and soft. Your eyes light on fennel, a little seed filled with licorice and mint kisses. Yes, this will pair well with your other leaves.

Each addition to your bowl is the promise of a new healing elixir that will float from a steaming cup and into your soul to mend, to cleanse, to ground. And though you started with your jars and only a vague sense of needing a cup of wellness, you find that after your blend is made and steeped and drunk, what you needed was time in the kitchen. Time to unscrew the lids on those jars of herbs and play with nature's medicine cabinet. Time to let your mind drift, to let the taste of rosemary settle on your tongue, and to have no other aim but to blend.

The Story Eater

That is all you want to do lately: gobble up each story as it unfolds, slurp up sentences like strands of spaghetti, feel the tang of so many words sharp and full on your tongue like the lime slice to your shot of tequila.

Some you want to savor as you would an artichoke, tearing off each page and running your teeth along its fleshy insides until you reach the heart of the story, one part thorns, the other ripe flesh. It is the process of tasting your way through that earthy labyrinth as much as it is finding the tender center that fills your soul. Others you would nibble at, like a wedge of fine cheese or a square of dark chocolate, loath to rush through the velvety decadence. And some you have no patience for. You toss their thick words and empty plots aside like so much wilted lettuce for the compost so that they may nourish your future words if not your present self. You know not how, only that all composted things must.

Then there are the ones you must devour in one sitting. Those ripe peaches, whose early blush make you unable to suffer through the tender courtship of each chapter, parceled out over a series of days they would require to fully digest. Yes, these you must bite into and greedily consume their fruit, thinking only after, when you are left with a listless paperback, that you should have taken your time, knowing full well you couldn't. Only it would be something to read this part or that again with virgin eyes.

Still others you turn to time and again, the familiar comfort of a well-trod plot as with the perfume of crushed garlic and rosemary staining your hands. The sharp scent of things simmering on your stove, an invisible ink absorbed from the pages of those stories, to later flow from your own pen.

On Summer

It is long days and even longer nights, as if your body knows that you don't have to be up early in the morning, even though you always are. The days stretch out before you as you fill them up with early morning walks before the heat takes over the city, drenching it in sweat and light. It is the quiet afternoons spent reading a book and drinking homemade lemonade under the protective shade of your favorite tree; the weekend evening spent sipping a gin fizz in the backyard while something sizzles on the grill. You have the luxury of getting swept up in impromptu picnics and long naps. Even your writing routine is broken up by spurts in the kitchen, making jam and pies and breads to use up all those peaches.

That one word, summer: a season of staying up late to stargaze, or read even more, abandoning yourself to the simple pleasure of getting lost in a book as you would when you were younger, snuggled deep into your comforter with only a dim light to help you read the words on the page. And when the monsoons come, you indulge in Gothic novels, the wind and the rain and the lightning outside echoing the mystery and mayhem between the book covers until your eyes close against your will and you awaken to a quiet morning, hushed in the wake of the previous night's storm. The rain, violent as it is, acts as the cooling force that tempers the day's slow sizzle. You revel in these contrasts; each day a symphony of heat and sweat, allowing your tomatoes to ripen on the vine, the night a monsoon song to soothe a parched city.

Time does not matter in the summer. It unwinds itself slowly from the clock of your everyday life, loosening itself from the tick-tock of 1-2-3-4-5 ... like a ribbon unwinding from its spool. The hands on the clock face no longer needing to clip through each second, for during summer the seconds expand, holding you there longer than you ever thought possible. And when it seems you are doing nothing and time is still, that is when you are busiest of all. Summer is a conducive season for imagination and dreaming, after all. Though in truth, you say that about all seasons when you are lost in their embrace. Much work gets done in an afternoon spent daydreaming, much created in watching the sun set.

You can give up real clothes, too, and proper meals. You are allowed to walk around barefoot all day, blades of grass kissing the soles of your feet, your hair loose around your shoulders and faded to a golden-red from the sun's caress. Your summer uniform is nothing but a loose dress or similar, anything that won't get in the way of you being you. Makeup is forgotten in favor of naked skin, the sky, the air, the earth touching your bareness. And proper meals, you don't need them. Lunch is an overripe peach eaten in the grass, dinner a slap-dash meal of sliced tomatoes and basil. Who needs anything else? In the space between putting away your last schoolbook and the dawning of the solstice, you have become a wilding, at home in the rich soil of your garden and the fertile dreams of your bed.

Summer. It is when you can abandon yourself to your reclusive nature; give yourself over to the bird's song and the chanting of the cicadas at night. You can dance with the moon and twirl under the sun's gaze. You can fill your lungs with the lush rose's sweet perfume and run your fingers through the wildflowers – daisies and dandelion heads mostly – and relish the way the clock's *tick-tock tick-tock* is replaced by the humming of bees and the rustle of leaves. For a season, you are unadulterated hedonism.

Cruising to Work

The sun is just breaking over the mountains.

Each building, each tree, each lamppost seems to spring to life under the playful prodding of the morning light. It is only you and a few brave souls gliding through the streets at this early hour. Streaks of liquid watermelon are painted across the sky, punctuated by tufts of yellow-cerulean clouds and the heavy purple shoulders of the Sandias. It is as if the mountains pull you toward them, toward the sun, with their magnetic force. Fingers of light seem to snake through buildings and illuminate the sharp green of barely turned buds on tree branches.

Your body sings with the bright energy of the morning as yet unblemished by time. This clean slate is tickled by the sound of country music wafting over the radio and the heavenly scent of your piñon coffee hot in the thermos, made the cowboy way: strong enough to stand a spoon in. Your favorite song comes on, and you crank it up just a little louder, waking up that last sleepy part of yourself as you sing along to the twangy tune.

In this moment, you feel like a true New Mexican, as you crank the music louder still, letting the rhythm wash over you like the sun's rays, feeling your dangly coral and turquoise earrings slap against your cheeks as you bob your head. Your foot presses the pedal just a little more, revving the engine as if in time to the beat of the music. The morning is making you bold. You greet this workday as you do every other, with the ritual of cruising down your streets, the streets you've known all your life, the streets that carry you through each hour of your day.

You signal to turn into the parking lot of your work, stopping just short of the mountains, the sun. You lower your radio. You must keep up appearances of being a serious professional, after all. You turn off the engine and emerge from your car ready to take on the world.

Things that Make Me a New Mexican

It is the way my bones seem to be made up of sun and clay, formed out of days curing in the desert heat. The way I can see the landscape made up of infinite colors: ochre, mica, taupe, and sienna. They are layered together to form hills, plateaus, dried-up riverbeds carved into the land, into my bones, dipping down into valleys and caves. A stunning wildlife that is never still, never just brown, never just layers of settled dust.

It is the smell of pinto beans cooking on the stove and the necessity of homemade tortillas. Are those store-bought discs worthy of the name? It is understanding the difference between *chile* and *chili* – the former in my blood, the latter, a sacrilege. It is knowing that tequila and tamales are the best medicine, though I can find my way around the herbs in my garden, a gift from the *curanderisma* running in my veins.

And then there's the turquoise. It has taken over the sky, filling up the city, corner to corner like the desert air fills up my lungs, chasing out the soul sickness that settled between my ribs when I lived – briefly, the desert always called me back – in a damp, dark place. Plus the sun. Always the sun. Always the sky that goes on forever, making it impossible for me to hide from myself.

It is in my collection of rocks and crystals, each stone a link in my connection to the land, and the faint smell of burning sage in the air to cleanse my home of stale energies and chase away bad spirits. It is in the bright colors that will always call to me. In the different colors that make up me – brown, red, white – never quite at ease with each other, and yet part of the same soil from which I was birthed.

It is the sun I must have, and the wide sky above me, and the desert earth beneath my feet. Only then am I whole.

Things that Make Me a Burqueña

Soy de Burque. Me. I am of these streets and this sky.

It's in my love of big earrings and cruising down Central. Though my car, much as I love her, will never be tricked out quite like those classic chrome peacocks lovingly restored and paraded up and down that old main street on Sundays.

It is in the way I can feel the magical and mystical permeating these streets as if the land were infused with an otherworldly essence, completely at home in this off-the-map desert town almost too big for its boots. The people, too, are a little off the map, valuing good food as much as good karma, chakra-opening yoga and mind-opening microbrews. And ladies, I love that we are a rockabilly raza. We are at home in that 1950s polka dot dress because we know how to take things that once made us powerless and forge them into frilly armor – all the stronger for its ferocious femininity. We found our wings in wing-tipped eyeliner and fat hoop earrings because that's our history too. We find power in that subversive mix of honoring (questioning?) our history as we question (and honor?) our Right Now.

We aren't afraid of the grit from our past or the possibility of our futures; however we find it, from the dealt tarot deck or a palm's riverbed, we know the history written in our blood and the future prophesied in the movement of stars across the night sky. What can't we do now that we will no longer be silenced? Watch and see how strong Bronze can be.

Soy de Burque. My favorite big, small town where the best places to eat are usually in some old adobe or parked next to a big red tractor, and you can find someplace to salsa dance every night of the week. What is life without swaying hips and the sweat-inducing beat of bongos? It is because I cannot live without freshly baked bread from the local panaderia or roasted piñon in winter when we are graced with a good harvest. And because I could never stay long in a place that doesn't understand that I go both ways – red *and* green – and never in a city, never with a person who doesn't know what that means. You see, I am drawing the battle lines with that last sentence, outing all those souls who like it mixed.

I need to feel the beating heart of this city as I wake every morning and go to sleep at night, feel the raw power of Mother Nature – the Rio Grande, the Sandias, the cottonwoods – nestled alongside our asphalt streets and mud houses. I take pride in the fact that my freeway can touch the heavens as it bends and curves over the city in a blaze of turquoise and concrete.

And again, I cannot say this enough, after leaving and learning that not everyone is molded from the bones of a dry riverbed. It is in my love of the people, warm as the sun that bronzes our skin. We live with an unapologetic ferocity, wearing our passions – those messy, violent things – like badges of honor, like cherry-patterned dresses, refusing to be silenced, refusing to be anything other than loud, open, dancing, breathing bundles of humanity.

Me. This city is me. Soy, soy de Burque.

On Mondays

They are the ugly duckling of weekdays, lacking the glamor of those carefree Saturdays or the flirty hope of Wednesdays, winking and hinting that the weekend is just around the corner.

But Mondays. Mondays. If you are willing to peel back the beat-up exterior, like scraping off long-faded wallpaper from suffocated plaster, you will find the fresh patina of promise. A crisp green frond unfurling into the workweek, delicate leaves licking possibility. The days are as yet untouched by overtime or unexpected obligations. You only feel that get-up-and-go, the product of a well-rested weekend and that first cup of coffee. The fire in your belly is fully stoked, the pep in your step like a quick foxtrot. Or better yet, a cha-cha.

Oh, Mondays. They are unabashedly ready for the bustle and industry of the week, leaving long naps and late nights in the wind as they jump and dance through the day on a full battery. You are completely recharged, gliding through your day, ready for anything. You have not yet begun to feel the gentle tiredness in your body and mind as you do on Thursdays, a sign of a week done well. You can do anything: write that extra page, go ahead and finally hang that painting, or weed that overgrown patch of garden. Or throw caution to the wind and go out dancing. Because Monday is when you can look at the world like it is brand new and yet deliciously predictable.

You know Mondays are one of the great unsung pleasures of the world. Too often lost in the shadow of the weekend, its louder, flashier siblings with frothy adventures and hedonistic impulses. But Mondays, Mondays. They are the dependable pleasure of your afternoon cup of tea and your evening yoga, your daily walk and time at your writing desk. They welcome you home with a bowl of soup at the end of the day and allow you to find grace in the homey task of washing dishes.

Mondays. They merely go about their business, asking only that you sometimes pause and take in their quiet possibility.

Visiting the Herb Store

You feel like you've stepped into an old apothecary shop.

The rustic sign outside the door beckons you with promises of wellness, while the crystals hanging in the window, winking in the gentle sunlight, seem to whisper a greeting to you as you cross the threshold into the store proper.

It smells of dried sage and spices; it is cool and a little dark inside to protect the herbs, but also a welcome respite from the desert heat. Your heartbeat seems to slow in this tranquil space, your shoulders loosen. Deeper into the store you will find shelves lined with jars upon jars of herbs, dried flowers, gnarly broken-down roots, and strange powders. Red, green, and gray clay. Salt so fine and pink it looks like fairy dust.

You run your hands across these vessels, marveling at the wealth of healing magic birthed from the earth. Each herb is a little miracle, made from dirt and sunlight and water. Tiny seeds brought to life by sheer willpower and raised through the earth for no other reason than a desire to see the light. These fine specimens contain the life force of all they sucked in through their roots, all they absorbed through their leaves. You can feel the power radiating from each jar, each root or flower carrying a distinctive energy.

You have a list of herbs you want. There is the fuzzy comfort of raspberry leaf for women's health, along with the mellow song of hops and skullcap for a sleepy-time tea you are working on – those somehow always conjure up images of pajama-ed bears, reading fireside on the old tea boxes of your childhood. But you aren't above being seduced by the jar of nettle leaves, the prickly fiend known best for its sting that is, at heart, a gentle tonic for the system.

You also get taken in by rosehips, more robust than the fragile petals of their flower, an unsung nutritional powerhouse. And you can never come here without wanting more of eyebright's gritty sparkle, all the better to see the world with. Then there is the lavender, those tight buds you will stir into your soaps, which takes you to the small case of essential oils nestled next to a display of multi-colored candles promising clarity, abundance, and love with just one kiss of a match. But it is the oils you want to burn, to perfume your house with the bright song of lemongrass in summer, the soothing musk of cedar in the winter, or the clean medicine of eucalyptus when your heart needs mending. You bypass the smudge sticks, as heavenly as all the bound sage smells, knowing that your half-burned one sits at home ready to smoke out negativity with the lick of a flame.

At last, you bring your jars and oils to the counter. Watch as the herbalist measures out your selections, marveling that no ounce looks alike – the rosehips a small pile, barely more than a liberal pinch, the raspberry leaves a mossy heap – and retrieving your chosen oils from a stash behind the counter. You can't wait to get home and unpack your little bundles of herbs and pour them into your own jars, your own collection of earth's healing magic.

Watching the Robin Build Its Nest

It is far too cold out this morning for it to feel like spring. Certainly too cold to muster the energy for the gardening plans you had been only too eager to work on when it was warmer. You try not to think of the increasing to-do list: laundry, cleaning out that junk drawer, finally organizing the spice cabinet, sweeping out the patio … The more you think, the longer the list gets and somehow feels heavier with the return of winter. Your breath streams out in thick white clouds before you as you venture out to your patio, your bathrobe wrapped tight around your waist. You feel winter's fingers hugging the earth one last time before wistfully letting it go. As if winter knows that as soon as it's gone, nature will turn to another lover, spring, where it will happily settle into the new season's warm embrace.

The robin in the tree, however, feels none of this. For this bird, winter is already as good as gone. And so it flits from tree to tree, gathering brittle leaves and other ephemera to build its nest. *Spring is here. There is much to do.* You can almost hear these thoughts swirling around its head.

You watch this bird swoop down to the ground, gathering dried grass in its beak, hopping over the empty fountain, in search of stray bits of thread and fluff for its new home. In the cold that is almost too much for you to bear, even with your fuzzy slippers on, you can't take your eyes off this bird as it takes its treasures. What others might see as debris and nature's cast-offs, the bird builds itself a shelter nestled in the crook of two gnarled branches high up in the tree outside the window framing your writing desk.

The robin builds its home tenderly, tucking dried grass here and there into the folds of its perfectly round nest, fussing over the sticks and leaves that make up the plush foundation of its little dwelling. Busy, busy. The home must be built, for soon it will be time to settle in and lay those eggs, to care and nurture new life. There is no room for hemming and hawing, no respite for tired bones, only the industry of creating livable beauty out of lint and pine needles.

Finally, the cold and lack of coffee get the best of you, and you make your way inside, but not before you cast a glance at your potting soil and seeds in the corner of your patio. Soon you will tend your plot of land, too. You will flit here and there, gathering supplies for your garden. But today you will care for your home. That to-do list is suddenly more manageable when you think of the robin. You will fuss over the arrangement of your spices, carefully fold each item of clothing, and tidy your catch-all drawer (no junk there, as it turns out, only seldom used but necessary matches, candles, rubber bands). And after you sweep out your patio, you will even leave out bits of dried plants and thin strips of bark for the robin.

A Trip to the Bookstore

You hadn't planned on visiting the used bookstore (your favorite kind) today, but you should have known better; an OPEN sign and a window full of books are always more than enough to lure you into the waiting embrace of any bookstore, if only for a moment. You should have also remembered that you find exactly the books you are looking for on these unplanned visits, never on the trips you deliberately pencil in. It's a little known cosmic rule that when you forget to think too hard about your list of desired books, the ones you've been waiting for – and the ones you didn't know you needed – will fall right in your lap.

When you first walk into the store, you can feel these stories reaching out to you, as if you could wrap them around you like a blanket and disappear inside their covers. You have long outgrown the notion that everyone feels this way about bookstores, about books; not everyone wants to nourish the imagination nor indulge in this portable feast for the senses. But for you, that nourishment is life. Your internal life, often a thousand times louder, more vibrant than your waking one. Though you find with each passing year, a better balance is struck. What's the use of all these stories if you can't use them to find – *live* – your own?

At first, it is enough to enjoy the mere presence of so many books, so many stories pressed together. There you are, running your fingers along the worn and well-used spines, taking time to pour over each section of this house-turned-store. There in the old kitchen sits philosophy, over there in a would-be pantry, the classics, a dollar a piece. In many ways, they are your closest friends, these books; your ever-constant companions made up of paper and plot, ink and characters, imagination and glue. Sometimes even held together by needle and thread in much the same way your dress is. Their spines are a familiar weight in your hands, the soft leaves stamped over with words like parts of a continuously unfolding oracle. The smell of the books – a heady scent reminiscent of lightly smoked tea leaves and history – is a soothing perfume, as is the feel of them in your hands.

It doesn't matter what it is. A worn fantasy novel, the bubbled letters on the cover almost completely worn off, though the epic scene below the title remains surprisingly intact; the slim, nondescript volume by Colette almost lost in the crush of the bigger books around it; or the vintage pulp books whose titillating covers alone could keep you occupied for hours. You find advice you didn't know you were looking for in the folds of Rilke, and another on women readers by an author whose name escapes you the moment you set the book down on its shelf – the name forgotten, but not the wisdom.

They all promise to lead you where you need to go simply by making you turn one page after the other and travel deeper into the realm of words. Nothing in particular catches your attention. It is enough to be surrounded by these friends, to walk the narrow aisle and get lost in the piles of stories, so crammed together it is almost as if their contents bleed into one another, create new narratives to fill the shelves. It is enough to fill yourself up with the possibility of these stories.

You spend more time in a closet-turned-sword-and-sorcery den but don't get swept away until you find a rack of vintage pulp books in what would have been the dining room. The kind with lusty dames and robust fellas on them, each with their own provocative tag lines: *The brilliance and wickedness of London's lustiest era!* or *A searing novel of a girl in trouble!* You're a sucker for those splashy covers and tawdry tales, always have been even before school officially ended your love affair with Serious Reading. The covers, well, you know the kind of pictures they like to paint. They are the cold, hard promise of people behaving badly – and liking it as much as you love reading about it. You finally settle on a pulp beauty to add to your collection about *the history of an audacious young seaman ... who dueled and prayed and sinned his way to magnificent adventure ...* Or so the back of the book tells you. Now these are the books that throw virtue out the window, just as they reject any pretense at literary grandeur in favor of grit and sin and a yarn spun so well you're dizzy after reading it.

But it isn't until you are almost out the door with this find that you stumble upon a shelf of cookbooks in what might have been the front parlor. This house was surely built in the days when there were formal and informal sitting rooms. You find yourself face to face with a row of books you have been in search of for some time – and a few you didn't know existed. There, stacked together like old cronies, is your long searched for *The Nero Wolfe Cookbook*, a must have for any fan of food or this classic mystery series, and a collection of M.F.K. Fisher and Julia Child books you simply must own. These women of food and words, much like yourself, feed your soul and your mind as they excite your palate. They remind you to be playful and brave and always ready to taste whatever delights the world has to offer.

Yes, you must have these. And the *Gone with the Wind Cookbook*, too, for much the same reasons as you need your swashbuckling pirate pulp adventure, for the cover and the idea more than the story or a recipe for classic Southern grits. It has been some time since you've given yourself permission to judge – enjoy – books by their covers. And then there is the novel about cheese and something whimsical; you don't know much more about it but that it must round out your collection much the same way a wedge of Taleggio rounds out a cheese platter. It has all the makings of a perfect bubble bath read. These you sweep into your arms, unable to curb your hunger for such tasty reads.

You can already picture your afternoon with your new books spread out on your bed, a tea tray sitting next to you as you flip through one and then another book, lost in a myriad of worlds, feasting on new ideas and images and experiences. These books, this feast of pulp and culinary musings and tributes to perfectly imaged worlds are a reflection of you. You are a creature made up of good books and good meals, food experiments and word experiments, usually with a side of wine and cheese.

Confessions of a Flower Eater

You would grow a garden in your belly if you could, so that your insides are blossoms, full with pollen and thick seeds, strong roots and liquid sunshine. This, this is your confession: You want to be part flower, blossoming out of the seeds resting inside your stomach.

It is true. They could infuse their spirit into your skin, and in return, you would give them a home. Just a tablespoon a day is all it would take, you think, as you gaze out at your flower garden, that alchemical blend of growing things and medicinal petals. So you collect your happy marigolds and nasturtiums, your puffs of dandelion and your bright tulip bulbs, your bright lavender and lush rose petals, and you begin the task of making your meal. You could grind them up with your mortar and pestle until each bloom dissolves into a thick paste, a murky drink not unlike the sludge in your compost. But where is the fun in that? How can you delight in the feel of seeds down your throat or a soft petal kissing your tongue? No, you want to feel the beginning of your garden in your mouth.

It must be a salad then. Decision made, you get to work, mixing up your flowers – seeds, petals, stems, roots – into an otherworldly meal. The tulip bulb is your base, thick and earthy, to welcome your eternal spring and chase away the darkness. Next, you stir in yellow marigold and passionate hope, then add peppery nasturtium, streaked with orange and red, to make you feel brave; dandelion follows, puffs, roots, leaves picked from a crack in your garden path, to echo your tulip base of infinite possibility. Add a few rose petals to dust the top, a delicate perfume to soften the aspirations of the other flowers. It is enough to enjoy the beauty of this moment. Your salad isn't complete until you sprinkle blue lavender buds across your feast, adding the final touch of tranquil healing.

You devour this salad, one bite at a time, crunching down on the meaty tulips, the melt-in-your-mouth silkiness of the rose, until there is nothing left on your plate but a marigold blossom, somehow still intact. You pick this flower up with your fingers and bring it to your mouth. You feel the feathery petals across your tongue, the way it falls apart under the pressure of your teeth, the weight of sunshine in your belly when you swallow it. This is your garden, each piece of your summer harvest preserved inside you so that you are now part flower, part hope.

Under the Influence of M.F.K. Fisher

It started with reading M.F.K. Fisher in a bubble bath, about her time in France and her search for the perfect martini there, of all things. She never found it but happily made do with a glass of rosé for aperitif. Before that, you were enjoying another unassuming Monday night, looking forward to a simple salad and turning in early to read and drink tea.

But then you found yourself under the influence of M.F.K. Fisher.

You simply couldn't shake the description of the pink-glassed aperitif or the lush musing on her first meals in France. The way food and wine served to punctuate the passionate episodes of her life. As the bubbles faded in your bath and your thoughts turned to dinner, your basic weeknight meal suddenly became an opportunity for more.

A quick scan of the fridge told you that there was still a half-bottle rosé and a few small wedges of cheese, not to mention the mountain of farmers' market vegetables. You must make aioli, you decided, to dip your perfect radishes in. And there is nothing to throwing together a small cheese plate of deep-veined blue and ripe Tilsiter cheeses and fat Castelvetrano and Bella di Cerignola olives. And why not put on some old jazz tunes so that the whispers of French love songs float through the air in time to your gentle whisking of eggs and olive oil? Soon, your apartment is transported to Provence and full of M.F.K. Fisher's joie de vivre.

The rosé was dry on your lips, tasting faintly of tart cherries, minerals, and ripe strawberries. You savored the ritual of whisking together your aioli, that perfect blend of garlic, egg yolks, and olive oil, as well as lining your plate with purple beans, radishes, and tomatoes to dip in your sauce. All at once your feast was ready, your Monday night turned into a vibrant celebration, a feast for the senses.

Like M.F.K. Fisher, you forgot about the world for a moment, about everything but this sensuous meal, simply prepared and enjoyed to the fullest.

On Camel Pose

You take a deep breath and stretch your body upward even as you kneel, shins planted firmly on the ground, the top of your feet glued to the floor. Your hands are your anchors, pressed soundly into your lower back.

Each slow sip of breath helps you reach higher into the sky until you must bend. Your spine curves in a backward swan dive; your chest is open, more open than you've dared let it be all day. The backward movement peels back the layers of each hour like fragile onion skins from your body. Slowly your hands fall from your back to cup your heels, grounding you so you can prepare for flight. Your arms have become wings that lift you from mundanity.

You can feel your heart beating through your rib cage, light seeping through the slats of your chest bones. A well of emotion tumbles out of you, some soft and subtle like a spring breeze, some black and tender like an ugly bruise. They start first in your belly, then travel up your spine, and pour out of your heart; it is a song you had forgotten you could sing. You are breaking and mending at the same time. Your throat tightens then opens, ready to receive the luminous gift – the breath, the song, the slow dance – of camel pose, releasing all that has been buried in your soul, covered in a layer of dust to be purged through your open chest, a ball of cleansing light.

On January

A paradox of thirty-one days. One month. One word. Too many resolutions and too little time to turn our attention from the previous year to the one already underway, pulling us along before we are completely done with our past.

Always divided with herself, torn between what was and what will be, just like the god she was named after. Janus, that divine soul whose features are split in two. She must forever keep her gaze on the river of time that overlaps and circles itself, so that a person may be at once here and there, simultaneously moving forward and stuck at a fixed point in the past.

Let its divisive nature be January's strength. When she tears herself from the strain of living the paradox of inward-looking winter and the promise of spring's emergence, let those ripped and ragged edges be filled with light. Let the gap that has emerged from the tensions between her reclusive nature and her desire to experience this world be a passageway, a doorway to another universe in which her contradictions are the stars that illuminate her path, not the stones in her pocket weighing her down.

And if she is lucky, she might even find nourishment in the space between one closed door and another, just waiting for her gaze to fall upon it so that it may wink into existence. Pomegranates, fat and full with garnet seeds, will sustain her as she travels down this new road. Each fiery drop she slips between her lips is a soul-seed sown deep within her belly to birth new intentions, sparks of light to guide her back to the eternal flame within herself when the nights seem darkest and the path split in two.

I Live in Stories

I live in stories.

They frame my world so that each turn of the corner is the prospect of a new adventure, each long-held gaze, a mystery to uncover. I hold on to the power of narrative in the hopes that it will shape my life, guide it along the paths of the heroines that have come before me. I want to taste and live and be bruised and revived and *shaped* by each scene of my life. I want to sew each turning point together into some semblance of a plot, that tenuous thread that turns ordinary moments into synchronous events. Look at my collection of beautiful moments strung like fairy lights across my consciousness.

I live in stories because I am uncomfortable anywhere else.

I am made up of the words and books I devoured as a child, and later still, as an adult. In my veins are the ink and pulp that shape the worlds I carry into my own. The spine of the leather-bound book on my desk is my spine, holding together pages upon pages of written memory with glue and vertebrae. I do not know how to be anything other than imagination and hope, and so flail, often wordlessly, hopelessly when I brush up against the literal – that heavy brick that does not know the meaning of wings.

I live in stories because I know that my life is a mercurial entity, always twining its way through this world in a curious expression of abundance and experience bound by the layers of what could be.

I live in stories because I know that I am a story.

Preparing a Dinner Party

You feel like Mrs. Dalloway on the morning of her party: fresh, excited, ready to relish everything from the flowers at the market to the bright red radishes you will pair with your Toscano cheese and gin gimlets for appetizers. You don a sensible outfit, easy to manage tunic and leggings – there is no time for anything with buttons or zippers – for a day of hedonistic productivity. Only a cup of coffee and toast for you this morning; you are too excited to gather your supplies to sit down for a proper breakfast. At the market, you take your time picking out the right bouquet, finally settling on the brash bundle of pink, yellow, and white wildflowers dotted with baby's breath, stems planted in a green mason jar. Then there are the radishes and root vegetables to gather, each bundle sending a giddy thrill up your spine as you drop them in your tote.

Home again, you get down to business.

It is best to begin with the tableware. You get to use your fancy dishes, the elegant salad bowl, a gift from your parents; the cheese tasting slate board, a new-home splurge; and the gold and teal cake stand, the perfect accent for your chocolate dessert. The table is set with a marigold cloth made by your mother, a hodgepodge of multi-colored plates and napkins collected over the years, and soft blue and green water glasses that you use for wine. You always thought the stems of those traditional glasses so fussy. Of course, your bouquet goes in the middle.

You are even pleased that your pantry is fully stocked, ready for an impromptu dinner party without much trouble. Your market trip was fueled by a desire for the freshest produce rather than actual need. It took only moments that morning to sift through the contents of your freezer and refrigerator and put together a menu of apple cider braised pork chops with early autumn vegetables, an arugula salad with pistachios and beets, a platter of artisanal chocolates. And of course wine. There is always plenty of that. Perhaps a robust Spanish Rioja will fit the bill. The next few hours are spent cooking to the soft crooning of Bebe and Gaby Moreno until your kitchen smells of apples and garlic and the joyful culinary mess is cleaned.

Menu complete, you turn your attention to your home. It is clean and tidy, as it always is. You must only tuck away your knitting and blankets, leaving your couches free for guests, and scatter a few extra chairs around, though you know they will be just as likely to find a cozy seat on the carpet next to your crawling niece. You pick out the records that will best fit the evening: Bill Evans, Dave Brubeck, Gerry Mulligan. They are the perfect backdrop for a dinner with family, mellow but festive, so they won't overshadow the laughter or the conversation.

Later, after a well-deserved nap and shower, you turn your attention to your person. A dinner party isn't a dinner party without a festive dress. You pull out a buoyant, cerulean A-line darling smattered with playful polka dots. It will compliment your red apron and glittery slippers admirably, though you know you will kick those golden shoes off sooner rather than later. Bare feet will always be your preference. You pin your hair up and fasten dangling pearl earrings to your lobes. Only then are you ready.

First, you put a record on. "Begin the Beguine" drifts out as you fill your home with warm light and put the final touches on your appetizer board, heavy with red radishes and creamy cheese. This is it. Your day has been dedicated to nothing more than crafting a celebration for those you love, you think, just as you hear a knock on the door.

The first guest has arrived.

Things You Do to Unwind

It is quiet. Your home, a blissful sanctuary after a day of noise and motion.

You slip out of your heels, feet firmly on the ground again. Your toes wriggle out the kinks of the day; the ball and heel kiss the carpet. You consider checking your email or reading, but your mind rebels against sitting at the desk, taking in more words. It is a hard task, but one of which you've learned the importance: letting your workday be done.

Your body wants movement. The deep pleasure of yoga asana that lets your form unfurl, releasing the paperwork and students' questions with each spinal twist, until your limbs, like petals, are loose and soft. It was a full day and a good day. Still, you know you need to transition from work to play just as you require the morning cruise from home to classroom.

The silence is broken only by the click of your jewelry as you begin the task of removing your armor. One by one, each ring goes back into the jewelry box, each a piece of the day washed away from your skin. Your earrings go next, taking with them the sound of copy machine and sputtering coffee maker. The war paint is last. Off go the mascara and blush that separate you the teacher from you the you.

But you are not quite ready for the mat. You tend your plants. Drooping basil is eager for a cup of water; the mums want only to have their dead leaves plucked from their underside. In the kitchen, you chop up root vegetables and put them in the oven to roast. You light a candle. You turn the kettle on for tea. Each act, a simple ritual of letting go of the day and welcoming the evening. Slowly, you begin to feel your mind drift away from lesson plans toward nothing in particular.

It is in that moment that you finally turn to your mat. Your home is fragrant with cumin and roasting vegetables. Your body breathes a sigh of relief to be away from the desk and onto the mat. Your only focus is on the breath moving in and out of your lungs, expelling any lingering stress, and taking in the beautiful moments that will carry you through the rest of the week. You relish the inevitable finish to this transition, after grounding mind and body, when you crawl into your favorite cozy pajamas, your soft second skin, to just be. The sun has officially set, and you can now welcome your evening with grace and gratitude for another day well lived.

On Saturday Mornings

The birds and sunlight wake you up instead of the too-eager alarm clock that usually intrudes upon your sleep. You linger in bed, the soft, knitted blanket a cozy hug around you, relishing the open day before you.

It entices you with its lack of a real schedule, and as you mull over potential plans, you resist committing to any firm blueprints for your Saturday. That would be sacrilege. In fact, the only thing you're ready to commit to is lingering over a strong cup of coffee on your porch this morning.

There you let the sun's rays wash over you. You stand firm, the better to soak up the light, like a desert lizard sunning itself, not wanting to move for fear the warm rays will roll off you like a soft breeze instead of sinking under your skin to warm your very bones.

It is entirely possible you will do nothing today. You say *nothing*, for it isn't the splashy outings and big events that weekends are so famous for – the ever-important social schedules that let others know how busy or important you are – but the solitary daydreaming and quiet reading of not-so-serious books, the conjuring in the kitchen or the writing desk. You may later throw caution to the wind and go dancing, feeling your body warm and soften under the attentive beat of congas, bass, and drums. So long as you don't pencil it in ... you can let the day speak to you. Nothing is more violent on a Saturday than those atrocious *schedules*. All this *nothing* nourishes the soul and heals the mind and body, allows you to enjoy a good martini in your pajamas on Saturday night without fuss or ceremony or indulge in that spontaneous dance.

Your mind returns to your cup of coffee on the porch. Your body is full of the sun's caresses, but your coffee mug is in desperate need of a refill. You turn your thoughts to breakfast –

something decadent, a treat after your weekday oatmeal – and the lush enjoyment of an uncluttered day spread out before you.

The Ritual of Tea

It is a symphony for the senses: The gentle whistle of the boiling kettle; the soft murmur of tea leaves poured into a strainer like grains of sand slipping through an hourglass; the first splash of hot liquid hitting the teacup; the fragrant steam washing over your face. You crave the ritual as much as the drinking. Need the carefully doled out tablespoons of silver needle or tightly furled oolong, and the time it takes to choose your cup.

And that first sip. Nothing compares to that first sip of a fresh cup of tea. The welcoming hot brew on your tongue washes away the wrinkles of the day. Your hands curl around your favorite oversized ceramic mug, enjoying the heat radiating from it, wrapping around your fingers like cozy mittens. It does not matter where or when you partake in this soothing ceremony – during a flurry of grading at the office or right before bed, or sometime during the day just because – only that you must.

You contemplate this as you watch your tea brew in a hand-thrown mica teapot, alchemy from your mother. The afternoon is sprawled out before you, a haven for sinking into your words and loose-leaf medicine. But you cannot tend the page until you have completed this ritual, until the first cup of tea is drunk, and you know a warm pot is there to fill it. You peer into this mica pot's open top to see leaves unfurling like tiny dancers gliding through the hot water.

Earlier you stared into your pantry, debating what tea to brew. A black tea would be the ultimate refreshing burst of energy, but you dismiss the dainty Earl Grey and smokey Lapsang Souchong before you because they belong to your office time. They are the beverage of Victorian ladies and Sherlock Holmes respectively, reminding you to move through your day with grace and awareness. No, you need something else now. Something as soft and loose as your hair around your shoulders, something that can keep company with your oversized cardigan and bare feet. You sift through your green teas, all promising that meditative calm and clarity, but push further still to your herbal blends. Not teas at all, really, if you want to be persnickety about it, which you don't. You want only the taste of healing tonics on your tongue.

It is the jars of tulsi and raspberry leaf that call to you. The holy basil promises to loosen any knots of tension in your shoulders, its fuzzy partner nourishing you from tongue to toe. They fill the pot with an earthy perfume and the promise of a well-written afternoon. Soon it is time to pour. You savor your cup while gazing out at the bare tree beyond the window framing your writing desk. And when the tea is gone, your eyes fall to the empty cup. Stray leaves stick to the bottom of it, teasing you with glimpses of your future if only you knew how to read them. Ah. Now there is a story. Cup refreshed, you turn to your words.

On Rainy Days, Miles Davis, & Whiskey

Today was a day of steady drizzle. The kind you used to dread when you lived farther north and could expect nine months of this darkness; but today, it is somehow more romantic, cozier for its rarity. It brings back one of your few good memories of the time you lived in a land coated in fog and frost: listening to jazz, drinking whiskey, watching the rain roll down your window pane.

Those were moments of bliss, when after a week of work and trudging through that rain, you knew you could come home, put on some Miles Davis, and pour yourself a little whiskey. You could swim forever in the sounds of *Ascender Pour L'Échafaud*, the jazz record of all jazz records. The movie it plays soundtrack to is incidental, forgettable even. But that is not the case with that woozy, intoxicating drone that Davis teases out, hitting your system harder and faster than any glass of the good stuff – and all the more dangerous for its luxuriousness. No fire, just cottony bliss that soothes away the rainy thorns of the day and melts the frost building up around your heart, a side effect of living among the frozen.

You enjoy a similar moment now, somehow more wonderful than when you partook of this ritual during those long winter days in that damp land. Now you do not need to hold that record quite so tightly, nor seek the refuge of your home quite so hard to chase away the frost, nor, in truth, drink your whiskey so quickly. You are one with your land at last, as warm and as feeling as you are, as full of richness and depth as that soundtrack. Now you can afford to savor that fiery elixir, this one tasting of just-ripe fruit up front and parched earth at the back, coy like a desert coyote on your tongue, never quite letting you pin down its taste.

This rainy day calls to you, begging you to play that jazz

record, which you now realize you haven't played in so, so long. Too long to be conscionable. Even though the rain has faded into a mere suggestion of moisture and cloud cover, you are still drawn to Miles Davis, a glass of whiskey, and gazing outside at the world softened by jazz and drizzle. This time from the comfort of your patio. You no longer need four walls to keep out the cold, only an open door to let in the beginnings of a balmy evening.

The Body Beautiful

Your body is a story shaped by bone and wrapped in tendons and muscle. You are too often afraid of it, this story, afraid to pull back the skin and feel the histories imbedded in your marrow. How can you absorb all that flowing ink underneath the cover?

It knows no other truth but the physical, the raw power of experience. It is made up of living memories, proof that you are nothing but delicious nerve endings and pumping blood, feeling everything, holding back from nothing. You are each of its curves and scars, a moveable history of your journey through this world. The baking burn on your arm, faded now with time, a reminder that you sometimes burn too hot; the puckered quarter-sized mark next to your belly button, the necessary byproduct of adventures in uncharted waters; the smattering of beauty marks and freckles across your skin. All are parts of a tattoo mapping the person you have become.

Inside you is another universe still, a hidden map of the people you once were, the places you once lived. Coded memories that aren't even yours. Not even you can read it all, as if some parts are faded with time and others obscured by invisible ink. And deeper still are the tiny organisms, those world within worlds that make up you, though you cannot conceive of those tiny seeds all piled within your body.

Too long have you been asked to sit in your chair or idle away hours in empty stagnation to contain the power of your body, to silence these stories. But your body wants to move, to lift you from that frozen seat and see if you can experience, if you dare to experience, those seeds bursting to life inside of you. Feel them pepper your history, your memory with new life, new vines in your veins mapping new roads in your ever-evolving story.

Reading Late into the Night

You've lost track of time.

You know it's late, but you refuse to glance at your clock for fear the little green numbers will pull you out of the magic spell the book has cast over you. After all, there is work tomorrow. And you wanted to get up extra early to finish off a few homey tasks. Those thoughts have been pushed away in favor of the world before you. It is enough right now to enjoy the refuge this story offers you.

It's just one more page – to see what happens – yes, just one more. You should just finish the chapter – yes, that's a good stopping point – except you still don't know what happened to the heroine or if the hero will ever escape his captors. It only makes sense to keep going, let the words on the page run through you like hot water through a tea-packed strainer. How are you supposed to sleep until you resolve this? Who needs sleep anyway? *Me*, a quiet, tired voice inside you answers, but it is quickly silenced under the fast turning of the pages.

You are cocooned safely inside your blankets, the soft lamplight keeping sleep at bay. You know tomorrow will be better for a full night's sleep. But you know, just as well, that even if you were to put the book down you would only stare at the little cracks and lines in the ceiling and whittle away the hours speculating about what could happen, how your heroes could have done things differently. Why they didn't see the clues earlier, as they were so plainly laid out before them? Or better still, you would replay the best scenes in your mind (they finally kissed!) or plot their escape (through the roof with the help of a dirigible and sky pirates of questionable ethics).

So you read just a little more.

Truly, it would not do the novel justice if you were to break off reading at such a pivotal moment, as if you would suspend the characters in that scene, freezing them until you could return to your book, find that right page, and begin again. It is only logical. More logical than your investment in fictional characters battling made-up villains in an imaginary world – but Oh! What a world!

You press on, enjoying the naughty feeling of being up past your bedtime.

Your eyes betray you first. They droop and flutter, even as they try to squeeze in one last sentence. Then your hands, too tired to hold the book up any longer. Eventually, your head tilts to the side, one cheek on the pillow. But the story has not left you – only the page – as your dreams pick up where you left off and play with the loose threads of plot not yet sewn into the larger tapestry.

On Sundays

A day in the kitchen.

There is no other way Sunday should be spent. You linger amidst your pots and pans, oven and stove, concocting medicine for the week in the form of hearty winter soup for your dinners and lentils with roasted veggies for your lunches. You even tinker with your herbs and spices, lazily dreaming up another tea blend – a treat to finish off your evenings before drifting off to sleep.

It is a day of devotion to nourishing yourself and your loved ones, filling up your soul as you fill your belly, fortifying yourself for the week ahead.

A nap is in order while the soup simmers on the stove and the roasted veggies cool. You allow yourself to drift on the couch, an abandoned book limp across your chest. You relish the afternoon quiet and sink into the deep pleasure of no real agenda, no need to be on for anybody, no reason to wear restrictive clothing.

Tomorrow you will greet the world, ready for the noise and bustle – yes, even ready to wear real clothes with zippers and buttons on them. But for now, you let the smell of your winter stew tickle your nose, as your mind dances between the dream world and wakefulness.

It will be the promise of a bubble bath that inevitably lures you from the couch, and the ritual of homemade pasta for dinner that steals you from the delicious hot bath. The slow, easy pace of the day and luxurious family dinner will always be your restorative tonic to start the week.

Summer Solstice & the Strawberry Moon

I went moon bathing last night.

I wanted to coat my skin in the rosy glow of June's strawberry moon on this of all days, the summer solstice. You can love the light of the year's longest day. You can enjoy the way the sun's rays stretch from dawn until the last whispers of dusk, straining to reach the farthest corners of waking experience. You can admire the way the unabashed luster of the fading daylight makes the mountains blush deeply as if anticipating things best tasted at night. But you must not forget the moon. Or the stars.

And that is why I moon bathed last night. I wanted to honor how the full moon brought more light to this day of light, illuminating the thoughts and forgotten corners that would otherwise remain in shadow. Better to know what lingers under the stardust and hides beneath moon-kissed rocks. It is bliss to find that half-forgotten memory buried amongst my herbs; catharsis to finally rid myself of the pests that take advantage of the cover darkness offers. This is my chance to ask the moon for answers. It will not be this receptive again for another seventy years, and then, where will I be?

So I asked my questions – and she gave me answers. She filled my mouth with the full sweet taste of ripe strawberries until their seeds burst on my tongue. She washed my hair in a waterfall of her silvery light and rubbed my skin in the promising perfume of rose petals. She confided that now, midway through the year, is the ideal time to find my story within a map gifted to me by the constellations. She asked the cicadas to sing so that I may dance. And she told me – as the moon always does – to remember to dream. Deeply. Tenderly. With wild abandon. She bid me stain my fingers and thoughts and beating heart with her lunar liquid, tonight the color of berries pressed between lovers' lips.

Dream. Always. For the best things begin in moonlight.

The Daffodils on My Nightstand

They sit so cheerfully on my nightstand.

I heard them the other night, when they were still closed buds in my vase, slowly crackling and giggling as they began to poke out their heads from the paper-thin coat that held them in place. One crackle. Two. Then, as if the cautious opening of the flowers was no longer enough, they burst open, all sunshine and brightness, leaving their brown husks behind.

They are the first thing to greet me in the morning. A dose of sunlight before the sun itself is up. Big, bold petals cradle a loud trumpet-shaped center as if it were a fragile porcelain teacup and they, the saucer. In the middle of each flower sits the furry, pollen-coated stamen, perfuming my room with the sweet scent of spring.

They chase away winter, promising warmer days in flower-strewn gardens. *Soon*, they say, *soon*. Soon I will be able to pack up my winter coat and shed my winter layers like they shed their brown husks. Soon I will be able to walk barefoot in the grass and picnic on fresh radishes and sprouts and berries. Soon. But until then, I have them: that bright cluster of flowers on my nightstand.

On Farmers' Markets

You are a sucker for a good farmers' market. Just like you can't resist the temptations of a well-stocked grocery store. You go there wanting to be seduced by ripe heirloom tomatoes, heaps of ruby radishes, and, if you're lucky, tangled nests of garlic scapes in the late spring, or juicy peaches near summer's end.

It is best to go early, before the heat and the crowds bear down on you, before the tender greens and overripe fruits begin to wilt and soften under the sun's gaze. For now, you enjoy the early-morning coolness, a gift from the previous evening's monsoons that raged through the city. The sky is still coated in a blanket of clouds promising still more rain. The city is quiet, subdued.

It is good coffee you must have first, in order to browse through the produce stands; it will hold you over until you decide what goods you truly want to commit to. Its taste is dark and bitter on your tongue, tempting you to balance it out with one of the pastries piled high in several booths like edible artwork dusted with powdered sugar. But no, you aren't ready to commit yet. Not ready to give up the little thrill that blossoms in your belly with each temptation, each possibility.

As you wind your way through the stalls, you marvel at the jewel-like produce: amber carrots, emerald greens, butter-yellow corn heads poking through pale green wisps of silk and husk. You keep your eye out for pickling cucumbers. What is summer without homemade pickles? And another eye out for homegrown tomatoes, those culinary miracles – gone too soon from the stands – that need only your teeth sinking into their flesh to make a perfect meal.

When your coffee has dwindled in its cup and you have made the full circuit around the market, you know it is time to let yourself be fully seduced by the few items you can't stop thinking about. Time to give in to the temptation of peppery radishes, purple and green okra spears, and tiny cherry tomatoes. You return for your treats, already planning the week's meals, which all somehow revolve around just washing and eating these earthly treasures raw. At the last minute, you throw in a bouquet of wildflowers because market flowers always make your nightstand look so lovely, make your mornings so much more delicious when you roll out of bed.

With a full heart and an even fuller canvas bag, you head home, content with your treats, excited to spread them out on your counter in a cornucopia of summer pleasure.

The Breath

Sometimes it eludes you.

You realize you have gone an entire day taking only short sips of air through your mouth. It isn't until you feel the tightness in your chest that you realize your lungs have not had the chance to expand – in and out, in and out, a living accordion. You don't know when you stopped taking full, belly-deep breaths, only that now they have turned shallow.

You stop what you are doing and simply stand there. You close your eyes. And you breathe. A slow breath in; the air fills your lungs and makes its way down to your belly. Each rib expands. Your chest opens up, shedding the short survival breaths and the pinched feelings that came with them. A moment to stop at the cusp of your inhale to feel the thumping of your heart. Then you breathe out. Let a slow stream of air leave first your belly, then your chest, finally your nostrils.

You do it again, pausing between your inhale and exhale. Now you feel your breath not just in your lungs and belly, but your veins, your shoulders, and your fingers, still now for perhaps the first time today. It travels through each sinewy muscle, leaving life in its wake. It sings up your spine, a vibrant coil of Shakti energy. You feel it all the way down in your toes. They tingle and reach toward the earth, grounding you to this world.

And you move through your day once again aware, once again firmly planted in your skin, air filling your lungs one long, deliberate breath at a time.

Wear Your Fashion like Frilly Armor

You must go boldly into this world. Remember that.

There is no room for a shadow of doubt draped across your shoulders like a fox stole or shabby dresses shot through with holes, a by-product of not tending, mending your armor.

Announce yourself.

For you are a woman of fire and earth, unable to be silenced. Wear that passion like the shield it is; let no person afraid of flame venture beyond it.

There was a time when you thought what you needed was not armor, but protective camouflage. If you could only fade into the background, disappear into the woodwork, you would find your safety. But you have long since outgrown your need to dress in muted colors, in perfectly matched ensembles of various hues of nude or gray or that one non-color at home in dentists' offices so popular among the faint of heart. No. It only softened your resolve; in your attempt to disappear, you eroded not just your tough, leathery skin but the spark that made you *you*.

You no longer feel the need to fade into your surroundings. That was another lifetime ago, one you gladly shed in favor of your peacock feathers, bright as sin, strong as steel. There is no question: You must go boldly into this world.

For you, the real you, your wardrobe is a work of protective art like the symbols engraved on a shaman's necklace or the tattoos inscribed on the skin of a medicine woman. Each day you prepare your outfit as a painter would her canvas, tenderly, one brushstroke at a time. Or as a gardener determining which flowers to plant in an open plot of dirt, only to decide it must be a small grove of wildflowers in all colors, all types, the seeds thrown around with abandon. Not tough enough for you? Well then, you must not know the power of one seed carving its way through the earth or the potency of the energy infused in paint swept across canvas. Your outfit is a living, breathing piece of art made up of layers of bright colors and loud jewelry and unapologetic joie de vivre; there is the ferocity masquerading as vulnerability. There is your strength, the light that casts out the dark.

You must go boldly into this world without fail. Your azure heels and amber jewelry and purple dress and bright green scarf remind you of this. It is not enough to fade into the background, not enough to just show up to life. You must embrace it, bite into it with zest as you would a ripe peach. Take pleasure in pairing turquoise stockings with your blazing yellow dress, despite the consensus that too many colors are unrefined, for they remind you to be expansive like your desert sky and warm as the sun.

Go ahead and ignore the proclamations that gray is the new black because you know full well that pink will always be the new black. It is contagious, pink, like the smell of hope and newly opened roses in the spring. Cultivate your love of polka dots and retro heels. In them, you are reminded that there is power in play. You must wear your dress that makes you feel like a daisy, though not everyone likes flowers. Let it remind you of the strength it takes to eternally bloom. Show off your layers of bracelets and the rings lining your fingers; let them be the scales that deflect others' fear and negativity.

At the end of the day, your wardrobe is a walking advertisement for who you are, an embodiment of who you are not afraid to be. So even if gray is your pink and clean silhouettes are your frilly dresses, be at home in your choice. Celebrate it. There is perpetual strength in wearing your creed.

Yes, you must go boldly into this world each and every day.

The Wind in My Hair

Sometimes it is like thick cool fingers grabbing a fistful of tendrils. Today it is soft, gentle, the hands of a child braiding your thick coils together.

It won't let you be still. It wants you to twirl and dance the way it does, whipping around trees and snaking its way through the dry brush. This force of nature shapes everything, even the hard granite. The wind only wants to kiss away bits of silt that grind against the rock's back. That is how it feels today, a slow, consistent presence molding you into a better self.

Other days, it is pushy. A big flirt stuffing its long fingers between the buttons of your blouse and tugging at your skirt. It throws fits too, casting sand and pebbles your way when it knows it's not always welcome.

Still, in whatever form it takes, it will always carry away your burdens: the heavy heart, the endless to-do list, the crick in your back that makes your dreams feel smaller and smaller. The wind wants you to get tangled up and flustered and maybe even a little gritty-eyed, so you forget to hold on so tightly to the flotsam of your day, the small hard facts that you think make up your essence.

You are not the pebble in your shoe, it says. Or the number of tasks completed. You are the number of dreams you plant and the moments you lose track of as you feel the caress of the sun-warmed breeze tickling your knees.

So let it whip away the debris. Let it remind you that you are the hopes you tend.

Reflections on a Snow Day

The universe offers you a snow day. Canceled classes give you permission to throw your carefully scripted plans out the window. No need to be at a desk today. Your kitchen is calling you.

You make soup, so much soup, and pots of pinto and black beans until your home smells like comfort, and your freezer is stockpiled with spoonfuls of love for those days when you won't have energy to conjure it yourself. You even pickle beets against the backdrop of Spanish guitar music and once-naked tree branches dusted with tiny white pearls outside your window. It is as if the crystal blanket across the city has given you permission to care for yourself.

That night, you sleep under the soft kisses of snowflakes and awaken once again to a city cleansed of its busyness by ten inches of snow. You venture out into that wilderness, armed only with a strong cup of coffee and hiking boots, past iced-over streets and neighbors shoveling their sidewalks in their bathrobes and snowshoes. You move toward the park that looks like nothing if not an open prairie. The scent of winter and cedar-burning fireplaces fills the air, as does the stillness interrupted only by the chatter of birds oblivious to the snow piled atop their homes.

In a few hours, this quiet expanse will be taken up by kids rolling up snowmen and falling backward to etch snow angels into the earth. But for now, it is just you and a lone cross-country skier. You cannot help yourself. The morning has made you bold. You cut across the safer street paths where your feet can land between car grooves and into the unblemished snowfall of the park. You know it will take you calf-deep into the snow, and your shoes and socks will soak through. No matter. You are on your way to a blazing fire and hearty breakfast with your family. What is a snow day for if not plunging into nature headlong?

Later, after the snow is nothing more than a memory and puddles under the sun, you still soak up the gift of your snow day as you soak in the bath, piled high with bubbles as fluffy as the snowfall you trekked through this morning. For a day – two, really – the snowflakes stopped time, allowing you to tune in to what matters: early morning walks and luxurious family breakfasts, lazy schedule-free days and long naps.

The universe gave you a soul day.

Kitchen-Sinking It

You must get creative with the food you have, using it all up before you pack your bags and head out on your next adventure.

It took all your self-control not to over-shop at the grocery store, despite the perfectly rounded artichokes and thick stalks of asparagus staring you in the face. You bought only the bare necessities: coffee and wine. It took even more reserve not to go to the farmers' market. That would only lead to a fridge full of spring's bounty: tender spring lettuce, red radishes, and, with luck, garlic scapes.

You know you mustn't do that, hard as it is. Everything but the kitchen sink must go, so you pile your plate with all manner of strange meals. You are traveling soon – that phrase playing round and round your head, a constant reminder – and have to clean out your fridge of anything and everything that won't last till you get back.

It has been a series of creative lunches and kitchen-sink dinners. There was the breakfast omelet with one-and-a-half bell peppers and small wedges of several different kinds of hard cheese; the lunch of quick pickled carrots, radishes, and cucumbers; the simple dinner of crudités and aioli to use up those eggs and any stray vegetables at the bottom of your crisper. Everything must go!

Then there is the carton of half and half that you try to ration out across the next four mornings so you don't have to buy another and have it go to waste. There is the watermelon you had forgotten about, the one you intended to juice. A watermelon cooler must be made, perhaps several. You will diligently work on whittling down the contents of your fridge until it is nothing but bare shelves and butter, mustard jars, and a wine bottle.

It's as integral to your travel preparations as packing your bags and boarding that plane. Yes, this is kitchen-sinking it.

Returning Home after a Long Journey

You love adventuring, you do. But after days of touring several different countries and seeing so many sights, what you want right now is a long bubble bath in your own tub, glass of wine in hand, jazz playing softly in the background. You want to sit out on your patio and linger over your morning coffee. You want to sleep in your own bed again.

As you slide the key into the lock of your front door, you feel like Bilbo Baggins – there and back again – and ready to write about your adventures. But first, you want to feel your home around you once more. You breathe a sigh of relief as you close the door behind you and take in your familiar surroundings. Everything is just as you left it – the turquoise blanket you are knitting in a heap on your cranberry couch, your writing desk covered in books and painting supplies. The kitchen, spotless.

It is the garden you go to first; you want to see how your plants fared while you were away. Did the cabbage worms eat all your lettuces? Did the pea shoots get enough water? Is your cucumber plant surviving? Your plants appear none the worse for the wear, though you fuss over them all the same, trimming back dried leaves and watering their potted homes.

You then fill your home with light, pulling back curtains and opening the windows for fresh air. There is life here again! You go to your bedroom and stare longingly at your big colorful bed, the covers of which you can't wait to snuggle under. It will be nice to dream in your own space again. You take in the kitchen, looking fairly forlorn without a full fridge or something cooking on the stove. It looks as if dust has gathered there, after almost two weeks without use. You make plans to remedy that quickly. Grocery shopping must happen, new recipes must be tried.

You unpack slowly, pulling out each token you've gathered from your travels and taking time to decide where they belong in your home. The ribbons bought in London must go on the vanity table, the tea in the pantry. Later, you will hang your paintings of Paris, done by a street artist, bought along the Seine, in your living room. And you will place your magnets on your fridge alongside the others, some from past travels, some bought in a fit of pure whimsy.

As you go through this ritual of returning home, you feel your things, your creature comforts begin to wake up, your house stirring as if from a long sleep. It is pure pleasure to be back. The only thing left to be done now is that long bath.

Body Wisdom

Every day it speaks to you, sometimes even in your dreams. It speaks of long-held memories, some not even your own, buried deep within the tissues of your muscles, of the hope ready to spring into action coiled at the base of your spine.

It speaks to you about the wings making their way out of the crevice between your vertebrae and shoulder blades. It reveals the scars engraved into your hip sockets, scars so old you didn't even know they were still there until a movement, a memory stirs them up again. You can begin to release them as you would weeds from your garden, gently loosening their roots from your soil.

It is limbs and torso that tell you when you need to move, to dance, to release yourself, free yourself from the bonds of the day. And when you must be still, your body tells you to be still, still enough to hear only the beating of your heart, and the new seeds you planted, cracking open to lay down roots where weeds once were.

Buying a Bouquet of Flowers

You couldn't help yourself.

There they were at the front of the market, a riot of colors stuffed into tall tin buckets, each flower vying for your attention like some flirt with no self-control. It's nothing personal; she does it to everyone who walks by. The sunflowers and daisies call to you with their bright happiness, sunlight springing from their petals. The snapdragons and irises lure you in with their intricacy. The purple irises still tight in their buds, unwilling to blossom quite yet; the snapdragons asking you to play with their delicate mouths that open and close under your gentle touch, less snap and more fish-kiss.

You settle, finally, on a mixed bouquet for its compelling arrangement of pink daisies and purple mums and another flower unknown to you, but lovely all the same. These are punctuated by shy lilies, with all but one yet to bloom, and little yellow wildflowers that might not have a name. You don't need these flowers. Not really. They aren't the kind to feed your belly, nor serve a useful household purpose like the baking soda you later put into your basket. But there is something to their wild elegance, something to buying a bouquet of flowers that puts you in the mood for picnics and long afternoons reading outside.

They add softness to your day and more than a little grace. You can picture them now, nicely trimmed and tucked in one of your small mason jar vases on the kitchen table perhaps or your nightstand, ready to greet you with the sunrise. Like the ribbons you collect or the sea glass, your bouquet of flowers brightens your home, lifts your spirits, reminds you that it is okay – necessary even – to indulge your senses. True, they will eventually fade, and the water they sit in will thicken into murky green sludge, food for the compost. But while they are fresh and bright and colorful, they feed your soul and remind you that some of the best pleasures exist in the space between one moment and the next.

Drinking a Glass of Wine on My Patio

The day is at an end. I have turned my teacher clothes over for yoga pants and a comfy top. My hair is loose around me. My bare feet enjoy the feel of the earth kissing their naked pads. I have forgone my usual evening routine in favor of quiet time outside; I've missed this time outdoors, the simple enjoyment of feeling my heart beat in time to the rhythms of nature. All thoughts of school are fading quickly under the magic of the evening's cool air, the soft cooing of doves, and the chilled glass of white wine in my hand.

I sip from my glass, savoring the dry flavors of grapefruit and basil, echoing the bountiful pots of herbs before me and the small citrus seedling I am currently coaxing to hatch. The liquid rolls over my tongue and down my throat, just as the sun sets a little lower in the sky. This sweet nectar sits in the bubbled water glass, the color and luminosity of green sea glass. I know I should probably turn my attention to the evening news soon, but for now, I relish the simple quiet after a day of noise and bustle.

The city itself seems to be winding down for the night, relinquishing its fast pace for calmer hours as if it were a person, undoing its necktie before unlocking the front door. I take another sip of wine, appreciating how the herbaceous flavor warms my belly and loosens my limbs. For a moment, I am nothing more than me – a quiet soul, enjoying a quiet night. The hummingbird whispers its secrets to me, then hovers over an open-mouthed flower to suck up its love – the little bird's reward for delivering its message. It is gone as quickly as it came. In its place, the gentle drone of bees, oblivious to the setting sun, knowing only that there is no such thing as the right time to collect pollen; you must enjoy the bounty as it comes to you.

I take another sip and close my eyes. Underneath the mellow

birds' song and garden chatter, I hear the hushed murmur of traffic as people head home, looking forward to a hot meal and a couple of hours doing nothing. An onlooker might see me stretched out in my garden and think I was doing just that. Nothing. But what a pleasure to allow myself to be still while the rest of the world moves around me. A small smile plays across my lips at the thought. I take another sip of wine. What a delicious sensation to simply do nothing – nothing more than gazing out at the world from the humble perch of my patio, mind blissfully focused on nothing in particular, nothing but the gentle grace of a day coming to a close.

Kundalini Energy

There she sits at the base of your spine, sometimes a thick coil waiting to snake her way up your back toward your wings, other times so tightly wound she forms a nest, pulled down from her upward spiral by the worries you've absorbed throughout your day – so many of them not your own. Yet it would seem you are asked to carry them, as if you are surrounded by cuckoos wanting to bury their eggs in your light, among your carefully cultivated dreams so that you might take their seed as your own and they, they will be free of the burden of those unhatched futures.

Your vertebrae grow too heavy to reach your wings, too full for anything but to hold those eggs tighter, lest they spill from their makeshift home. Your back, too, feels the weight of this, as if these eggs are stones rather than another's hauntings. But your light is stronger than those leaded shells, your sleeping serpent ready to shed her skin, cast off these stories that don't belong to her.

Slowly she begins to twist and contract, to wriggle and writhe, until each egg, each burden falls out of the sinuous basket at the base of your spine. You are left with only light-as-air hatchlings – all yours – made of hope and long hours on the mat. Made of focused intentions cured in your sweat, needing only the nourishment of a spinal twist to distill their potent magic.

She remembers what she is, your spine. Not a cuckoo's nest but a spiral of energy, always evolving, casting off all those memories from others or past selves until you are left with a love song. A dance between your spine and your breath, that upward moving coil, kissing each vertebra as she reaches for the light. *It is not your job to hold other people's pain*, she says, *nor their stories – only your own joy.*

Revisiting an Old Story

It's like a friend you'd almost forgotten you had, until you accidentally stumble across it one day in your search for something soothing to read.

There it sits, high up on your bookshelf, sandwiched between books you have read, those you will read, and some you'll never touch. There is the one that you go back to again and again, despite the many unread stories taking up space on your shelf and nightstand. It has not finished telling you what it needs to; you doubt it ever will. You only know that it calls to you periodically. And each time you peel back the cover, you find another nugget of wisdom in those well-worn pages and beloved passages. Some you remember time and again, others reveal themselves slowly with each additional reading as your life experience seasons your understanding of the story.

Just to hold it is like being enveloped by a soft, downy blanket. The edges of the book cover have been loved off. They are now only round, fuzzy layers of cardboard where they were once sharp, cloth-covered points. The spine is cracked and split on either end, carving deep wrinkles that begin to separate the book from its pages. Dog-eared corners prevent the book from closing completely and some – those oft-read chapters and passages perfect for a stopping point – have no corners left. So often have they been folded over to mark your place that they've been worn off the page without your noticing. The cover, too, seems to have permanent grooves where your fingers hold it up. It welcomes you as you welcome it, so well do you know each other.

Before you know it, book in hand, you are curled up on the couch, once again immersed in the world of your favorite characters. Each city street or hedgerow is so familiar, as if you have walked those grounds a hundred times before. You relish entering the familiar kitchen or the alchemical workshop as you would your home. If you could, you would spend a quiet afternoon there, sipping tea in front of the kitchen fire, or rummaging through ancient books and jars filled with mysterious things in that secret workshop. You would take time to converse with these complex creatures known as fictional characters, always ready to help you grapple with your life as a mere human. And you would take time to consider how you might fit into this plot, what new voice you could add to it.

You eagerly anticipate every plot twist as if it were a long-expected guest that you wait for from your perch by the window. There it is! The car has turned the corner and makes its way up the drive, signaling the arrival of your guest, just as the new chapter reveals what you already knew would happen, and yet, keeps your heart racing all the same. You read on, grateful to once again be in this familiar world, uncaring that soon you will reach the end of your book and have to put it back on your shelf – no, you try not to think about the end.

For now, you content yourself with lingering in the pages of your worn book, taking comfort in the old story that tells itself again and stretches beyond the page into your waking imagination. It is part of your soul now, a strand of story that has woven itself into the very fabric of your being.

Writing at the Kitchen Table

Sure, you have your own writing desk, one lovingly crafted over the years. You can still see evergreen where it bleeds through the turquoise you painted over it, a tribute to the expansive lightness of your beloved skies. The inevitable wear and tear of scratches and well-worn grooves where your feet rest on your chair are as familiar to you as the lines on the palm of your hand. And the scattered gemstones, carelessly placed daisies, and stacks of half-read books only add to this still life. A study of a writer's mind.

But sometimes, you need to forgo the creative splendor of that desk for the warmth and sanctity of the kitchen table. Here, you can spread out and make your journal and pen at home with the salt and pepper shakers. Your hands can smooth the wrinkles from the homemade mustard and ochre tablecloth strewn with embroidered vines and buds impatient to burst open; a gift from your mother. This homey task is a welcome respite for your fingers, much more soothing than finding their way around the roughness of each wooden groove and lost story on your writing desk.

The only music is the whistle of the kettle and the sound of you and your words breathing in unison. Perhaps there is even some stew simmering on the stove, perfuming your cozy space with comfort and garlic. There is no room for dainty teacups here, just as there is no time for a ladylike cup of Earl Grey. Only oversized mugs will do, enough to hold the rich brew you concoct out of oat straw, alfalfa leaves, and astragalus root. This is working tea. It fills you up with nourishment from the earth and protects you from the elements. Each sip brings you closer to the ground, where you write best.

It is easier to plant your letters in that mineral dirt and watch the words bloom. Their sun is the glitter from the mica mug from which you slurp your tea. And you watch with the pleasure of a gardener who has pulled the last weed from her plot of land, as those words unfurl into sentences and burst into story just as the tight buds on the tablecloth erupt into bloom.

Only at the kitchen table can you get your hands dirty and your mind clear.

Dreaming under the Supermoon

You were in my house last night, ephemeral tendrils of light seeping through my window and curling around my body as I slept. I didn't see you, but I could feel you sweeping away debris from my mind and old skin from my body, one gentle caress at a time.

You bathed and cleansed old wounds and shed light on the darker corners of my heart, allowing me to release myself from burdens I didn't know I was carrying. You held me in your arms as I dreamed deeply of things long past and those to come, of the here and now, and of the realms that only exist when I close my eyes. I would weave your light into a cloak if I could, so that I may wrap your arms around me whenever I need your healing embrace. I would bottle your light if I knew it could be contained, so that I might fill myself up with your lunar liquid when the light inside me seems as if it would expire. Like my crystals recharging under your care, I, too, need your wisdom to find renewal. Now more than ever.

After a week of letting go of old selves, of old ways of thinking, I return to my dream realms to finish the task of unburdening myself from people I will and never should be. You, Supermoon, help me with this, with your larger-than-life wisdom casting hope, rebirth, gentle understanding into the shadows of my home, myself. You bring me perspective, illuminating the smallness of my old identities, the arbitrariness of my worries as I move forward. Here I grow, as a seedling under the sun does, but I am a midnight bloom. Birthed in darkness, the stars our only witness as I emerge from your cocoon spun of light and realization.

You, dear moon, reinforce the necessity of gentleness in my life, of the internal feminine virtues so often undervalued in this world of loud and busy. No, you say, that is not your road. You silence the fury of *go-go-go* with the reminder that I belong to the earthly cycles – day to night, season to season, waking to dreaming – that they will guide me if I live beneath the surface of a world that thinks it has no time for the turning leaves. Foolish. We are all bound by the shifting skies. You tell me that I am a daughter of the moon, of the stars and midnight, of the quiet hours of reflection, the mistress of secrets revealed only in the hush of night. *Move inward,* you whisper. There I will find my answers, and then I will find this simple truth: As within, so without.

On Peaches

You were lured out of your home today with the promise of perfectly ripe peaches from the farmers' market. They are like August, lush and full of summer sunlight, almost overripe after a season of sunbathing.

It is the soft fuzz on their skin that you first enjoy. You roll your thumb over it as you grip a firm peach in your hand, the white down a gentle contrast to the red and yellow blush of its skin. You feel for firmness first, that tricky combination of ripe but not too ripe; everything needs a little give. It is a hefty weight in your hand that promises sweet juiciness without bruising or mush. You look for rose and mustard in their coloring, not the anemic wash of green butter and faded berry stains of a fruit plucked too soon from its tree. No, you want your peach full of life and juice.

You add perhaps too many peaches to your basket at the market, telling yourself you can always make a cobbler or pie, knowing full well your edible jewels won't last that long. You pile them carefully on top of one another so as to prevent bruising. When you get home, you just look at them for a bit, as if taking one out of the pile and sinking your teeth into it would somehow break a spell. As if this would make you forever hungry for this fleshy fruit, even after your happy pile dwindles to nothing under your voracious appetite and its season has passed.

But the feeling doesn't last long; that pile of ripe fruit is too tempting to resist. Eat one you must. You take the peach on the top, the one with its green leaves still attached to it and, without any attempt to control yourself any longer, sink your teeth into it, feeling the fuzzy soft skin break under the weight of your bite. Your mouth is flooded with the tangy-sweet taste of its juices, your tongue rolling over the velvety softness of its flesh. You don't pause long enough to enjoy that first bite or any of the others, but keep going, luxuriating in the way peach juice dribbles down your chin and hand. Finally, there is nothing left but the pit with only a few bits of yellow flesh sticking to it.

This – this feeling of ripe sunshine in your mouth and sticky hands, this is summer.

On Wings

You felt them growing underneath your skin right along your shoulder blades. Like new teeth ready to break the surface of your gums. The tender flesh around them throbs from the tension of keeping itself together, in spite of the determined winged blades forcing themselves into the light.

At first, you thought it was only tight shoulders, muscles that needed loosening. But as the pain grew and little bumps began to form on either side of your spine, you knew. And when the skin broke, revealing bits of blood and bone and feathers, you could no longer deny your wings. The pain wouldn't let you. It was all you could do to keep from passing out as they cracked through your surface, pushing against your skeleton to make room for themselves. They know no law other than expansion. Be free they must. You fell onto your hands and knees, holding on to the earth to keep yourself together as they seemed to pull you apart.

And here you thought you had stopped growing. Now they rest behind you, still sticky with your blood. They are hollow bone and fragile blue skin, pricked with the beginnings of feathers. Tufts of their down paste themselves against your back, along with flaps of broken skin. At their newest, these wings still span the length of you and far exceed your width; you could make your home in them, which is what you do when they've fully emerged. You collapse against the earth. Instinctively, they fold around you like a light-filled cocoon as you tremble and shake.

They grew, you now realize, out of hope and lessons learned the hard way, out of holding on and letting go. Nourished by the warm caress of the sun and a growing sense of self. Delicate, yes. Ephemeral spans of imagination and bone. But strong, unbreakable. The proof is in the way they pushed their way out of your back – not everyone can handle the weight of wings. And not everyone can see the expanse of bone and feather you now carry with you, though you tread more carefully as you learn to balance this evolution. They only hear the faint rustle of feathers. Only feel the soft breeze from flapping wings as you figure out how to move and dance with your new limbs.

And soon, soon you will learn to take flight.

Making Limoncello

It is your way of distilling sunshine in a bottle. Of capturing the salty, bright air of the Amalfi coast and the golden light of Tuscany. It will forever be your first time in Florence, savoring the sweet lemony digestif on the Palazzo Vecchio, only half-believing that there you were in the heart of a city you had only ever read about. It was midnight, and jazz music from a nearby concert drifted over the square. Spring had only just left the city, gifting you with cool evenings and the promise of summer. The tall glass of chilled limoncello tasted like the little bit of sweetness you'd been longing for.

The year had been like swallowing the sour lemon of your past one section at a time; now you realized the lemon was not the bitter pill you thought, but the foundation for future honeyed abundance. The chilled liquor before you was the fruition of what you thought was nothing but an empty glass.

You wanted to remember this feeling. This recognition that you could transform bitter skins into sunlight. You needed to know you could conjure this medicine whenever you needed to. So a recipe was concocted. You did not want to leave the light of your first trip abroad in another country but feel it daily in the life you woke up to every morning.

Now, as you peel your lemons, you think back to that first night in Florence and how smoothly that limoncello went down. A cool cleanser on your throat, the perfect antidote to a year of uphill climbs and dead ends. The heaviness in you had lifted, carried away by the soft breeze and kept away with the lively conversation of your late-night companions and the music floating across the piazza. It took the bitter peel of a tart fruit and a long year, and turned it into something soft, gentle, enjoyable.

You do this now too, taking those seemingly unusable pieces of your lemons and turning them into something beautiful. You work your way carefully around the citrus, making sure to shave off the outer skin but leave the too-sharp pith untouched; it will not do to let the bitter rind steep in your brew that is made up of light and fresh starts. It is a brew of new beginnings after all, with no room for nursed resentments. You peel enough to fill a mason jar and then drench that pile of yellow slivers in vodka. You must only use the ripest lemons to begin with, or your drink is spoiled from the start. The remaining lemons look half-naked wearing nothing but their white undergarments. You juice them for lemonade, the drink similar enough to the one you are steeping to hold you over until the limoncello is ready.

As the weeks pass and your mason jar full of lemon peels and spirits darkens to a rich golden hue, you consider the time it takes to make something worthwhile, to let it cure until it is ready to be finished off with sugar and water. Each morning, you begin your day examining the jar on your kitchen counter. Shake it up. Watch as the peels float back to relative calm. Remove the peels too soon, and you are left with a weak drink, more sugar than citrus; too long, and the fruit's oils overtake everything else, saturating your drink with the harsh taste of moonshine. The timing is everything. Only the golden color of the concoction tells you it is ready. It does not listen to the number of days outlined in a recipe or firm dates you've set in your head, but arrives at perfection in its own time.

Only the soft morning breeze carrying the faint whiff of citrus whispers that it is ready. You finish off the rest of your distilled sunshine, melting sugar in hot water, and then, while it cools, straining the lemon peels from your golden liquid fragrant with the zing of a summer day in Capri. Here is the perfect alchemical moment: You combine your syrupy water with the citrus spirits. It is almost done. Now it must cure again, this time in your fridge. The chilling process marries the lemony oils and sugar in a way heat never could. A perfect antidote for someone who always burns too hot.

At last, the moment has arrived. You are ready to try your first batch of distilled joy. Of course, it must be enjoyed after a homemade pasta dinner with family, once the dishes are cleared, and the day begins to fade into night. You pour the concoction into small ceramic cups no bigger than a shot glass. Limoncello is made for sipping, savoring as you would a sunset. You admire your first batch, almost hesitant to take that first sip. But when you do, it is perfectly chilled and reminiscent of those long, slow nights in Italy, unrushed, unfettered, the taste of sweet lemon and cool velvety luxury on your tongue.

It has been some time since your first trip abroad, but you continue to have a batch of this ephemeral drink on hand to honor your revelation that sometimes the sweetest things emerge from the sourest fruit.

Things I Want to Unlearn

They are like the tight laces of a corset, these lessons, cutting into your ribcage and squeezing the air from your lungs, taught to you by people and things that prefer you breathless – and so, unable to speak. Each tug of the ribbon wraps steel and bone tighter around your frame. Containing you. Small sips of air sucked through half-open lips are the only sign your heart still beats. Those and one delicious thought: a pair of scissors.

You could use the ones you have set aside for your embroidery. No bigger than the palm of your hand and engraved with bird wings. Silver and sharp. Stronger even than the metal jacket closing in on your pumping heart.

You give in to your impulse. Wrap your hands around the cool silver of the thin blades. You are alone. No one can stop you. Slowly, carefully, you reach behind you for the knotted tongue at the base of your spine. You almost can't slip the thin blades under the satin; the laces are so tightly pulled together. But you do it and feel the first lace pop loose of its eyelet.

There it goes …

… The temptation to search for the rotten fruit in a barrel full of blush-stained snow apples. All you need to know is that you have an abundant crop and faith in your ability to pick the best jewels from the orchard. You've been through enough harvests to know the difference between worm-softened cores and firm flesh.

Then another.

The flash of disappointment when you see your imperfect body, alone, at night, freed from the corset's confines. The puckered skin along your stomach, the shiny purplish lash along your arm, the bruised streaks where your ribcage pushed against the corset's skeleton all day, every day – and others, so many others – aren't scars. They are life lessons tattooed on your skin.

Trophies from the risks you took, the jumps you made, even the moments when you knew it was best to retreat into yourself. They are memories of times you dared to live beyond the narrow path someone else decided you should walk.

More air in your lungs. You can feel your chest expand.

Enough for you to reach higher and cut through another lace ...

... And there goes the bricks and mortar you once used to make a fortress for yourself. You called it a home, but the walls grew bigger and bigger until it felt like a tomb. A place to bury the pages of your stories. The ones that no one would read because they lacked the light that could spark them to life.

Let those bricks be reduced to rubble. Let your stories breathe as you can now. And find their own homes when you set them loose like birds to the sky. In their own time. In their own way. And remember that your real home is never behind tightly cinched, cloth-wrapped whalebones or mortared stone.

How long did it take you to remember that your home is in the earth and in the sky? That the roots of trees and flowers will always be your welcome bed, and the wind is there to sweep away the last cut ribbon from your cage.

Things I Want to Relearn

The curve of your own smile. Sometimes you touch your fingers to the corners of your mouth just to feel the way they turn up when the sun kisses your lips. You don't always believe that your body remembers how to express joy.

Then there's the bliss – more a memory now – of abandoning yourself to the woods. The city, a thing forgotten like an unremarkable story or adequate meal. Where is that spontaneous wildling unafraid to go deeper? The forest, be it in a book, heart, or landscape, is made up only of trees and dreams and roots and shadows, after all. And they all want you there, going so far as to lay down a bed of fallen leaves to pad your steps and cover their rocks with moss so that you may rest your head in comfort. It has been so long since you listened to their secrets. So long since you told them yours.

And how did that game go, where you picked your way across the stream, searching for the next foothold on rocks smoothed over by the water's caress? You weren't always thinking of snakes and eels hiding under them. You weren't always worried about slipping. There was only the cool, clean feel of the water lapping at your feet and rushing between your toes. Feel it now and let the wet ripples carry your worries away.

And you can't forget your hair, nor the times you wore it loose and wild – though some would call it a thorny thicket or a nest of copper wires – but those are voices best forgotten as you relish the way your curly, auburn locks cascade down your naked back and fall around your open shoulders. You must remember how to weave flowers into your long tresses, and let the only chains you wear be made of daisies.

Next, find those delicious beats that pull you toward the dance floor. Court your inner hedonist and let her play and laugh and move her body in the way that it was meant to be moved: in time to the heady heartbeat of congas and claves and vocal chords wrapped tightly around a melody. This is you remembering that your natural state is joy and that there's nothing wrong in sinking into a song's lusty embrace.

Perhaps by reclaiming these pieces of yourself, like stray strands of string and dandelion heads, you can begin to weave a new story unfettered by the dead-end plots that made you forget yourself in the first place. You never belonged at the bottom of a well or stuck under the heel of another's boot.

Weave together more forgotten things into this wild tapestry: scraps of bright ribbon and grapevines, bits of memory, and the feathered corners of well-loved books. Stitch it all together with those small pops of energy that tell you everything you need to know before logic tries to smother the sparks. Then, when you have incorporated your last fingernail and sage leaf, finish it off with the whispers of the universe – here in a dream, there in the roadrunner crossing your path – that ask you to remember, relearn, truly understand that you are a daughter of the moon.

That your life is in long fingers curling around tree bark, feet resting on thick branches, as you peer past the foliage into the endless horizon.

Celebrating Spring

The romantic in you wants to wear flowers in her hair and walk barefoot through the newly greening grass. The lover of fine clothes is eager to don her first flouncy pastel dress of the season. The earth woman wants nothing more than to plant the seeds heavy in her open hands.

You want to celebrate the seeds you've sown in the past year and the ones you hope to plant now. These pods cradled in the palm of your hand are the promise of a prolific year. A bumper crop of whatever you choose to give to the soil. You are intoxicated by this delicious itch to create new life, bringing dreams into the here and now.

Soon you will reap your first harvest of radishes – full of earth and pepper – and those little tender lettuce leaves, the product of your love and care. But what about your other seeds? The wish floating on the cottony dandelion wisp? Or the fertile black disk of a hollyhock, shameless in its pursuit of life? What of the hollow bulb, empty of everything save for a few fragments of a past life?

You must be careful which seeds you choose to plant, for now, under the light of the blood moon, the gaze of the spring sun, whatever you plant will surely take and grow strong in this receptive soil. The seeds weigh down your palm, the dandelion heaviest of all. You do not need more ghosts haunting your waking life, no memories of what was walking by your side. You crumble the all-but-dead bulb, consigning it to the compost where its remnants will feed your garden. You take that thick hollyhock seed and shove it deep into the earth, knowing it will reach to the sky and bring her sisters with it.

Lastly, you take that dandelion wisp, full of your wishing, and cast it into the sky. Let it find its own resting ground, its own soil to make its home in and grow full and strong in its own time. It will find its way back to you, as all wishes do, when you are ready for it.

On the Necessity of Good Coffee

The week before, you greeted the day with subpar beans bought in a moment of desperation. You needed to replenish your coffee stash but didn't have the wherewithal for another errand. So you settled for some regular store-brand beans. The days to follow would teach you how foolish you were. How necessary that extra trip would become.

You brewed your first pot from those unfortunate beans, on a day when you most needed a cup of rich liquid strong enough to put hair on your chest. What you got was a stale, brackish brew akin to hot, dirty water. It soured your taste buds and made your brain feel fuzzier than it already was. No. This was simply no way to start the day – any day.

You stared forlornly into your cupboard, as if it would take pity on you with your watery gaze and procure some tasty grounds that had been pushed to the very back, stuck behind cans of beans and jars of olives. But no such luck.

The day unraveled in a foggy plot to find a solid cup of coffee from school cafes and nearby stores. This one had gone cold sitting on the burner too long, the other brewed too weak, yet another thick as molasses and twice as cloying. Eventually, you gave up the hunt and committed to that one errand you now wished you had taken the time to run days earlier.

You bought your beans. You ground just enough for the next day, keeping the rest tightly sealed for freshness in your cupboard, as far away from the other offending beans as possible. The robust, chocolaty aroma perfumed the kitchen – a promise of tomorrow morning's pleasures.

The next day, you turn your coffee maker on, longing for this simple indulgence too long denied you. And there it was, a perfectly brewed cup of decadent goodness. The scent wafting from the mug, teasing you, begging you to take your first sip. And then another. And another.

No Is a Two Letter Synonym for *Yes*

You used to be so good at it – the *no*. But then again, you only thought you knew its meaning – as if it only ever had one. It took years to learn that within the *no* is a *yes* and a *yes* and a *yes*.

You would want to say it, feel those two little letters roll over your tongue and escape your lips like a soft exhale. It was a dangerous and intoxicating ability to brandish that one small syllable to protect your freedom. Perhaps you liked it too much. So firm were your boundaries that you had built yourself a fortress forever protected, forever isolating yourself from human experience. You began to wonder if that was the real purpose of the *no;* if there was not also room for a little *yes* in your life as well. Gradually, that fortress deteriorated, eroded by questions and the desire to feel fresh air on your face. You needed only a home, not a stronghold.

You wanted your *no* to be an expression of joy, cultivating the hollyhocks you so love and keeping out the poisonous spiders. You fumbled at first, figuring out how to balance the *yes* with the *no;* an ongoing meditation. Somewhere between leaving the fortress and building your home, you felt it growing inside you: the desire to let go of responsibilities and stories not your own, shedding them like heavy flaps of other people's skin you'd worn for too long, mistaking them for your own. All it took was one courageous whispered *no* to release you from the bonds of overextension. To leave more room for a little *yes* in your life.

You are beginning to understand this word now. You are not foolish enough to think you have or ever will learn all its mysteries: It is *no* to the fortress, *yes* to the home.

To the Everlasting Yes!

It is not the question that matters, only the answer. Put another way, the Why only takes you so far. It is the Yes, that glorious everlasting Yes that gets the job done.

The Why is full of too many uncertainties, tangled threads knotted into a heavy ball of your potential histories. What was, what is, what will be, and – strangest of all – what *might* be, those thin strands of chance that vanish and reform with every step in a new direction. It cannot be fathomed or untangled; to try to separate one cord from the rest is to further knot yourself up. Let go of holding on to those threads so tightly, and let them find their own way around one another until they are not a snarl of string but a rich tapestry of the adventures you take on.

And that is the reason it is not the Everlasting Why that matters, only the answer. Yes!

Yes to singing in the car on your way to work. Yes to sneaking in a midweek, midday yoga when you think you should be working. Yes to the impromptu visits to the herb store. Yes to watching the sun set. Yes to flirting. Yes to dancing in the moonlight. Yes to the simple, joyful moments that impregnate your day, those delicious morsels too often looked over in the hurry to get from here to there.

Yes, it is the Yes.

Yes to a good day at work. Yes to a well-planned day, and absolutely yes to the people who take you by surprise and take those plans in a different direction. Yes to feeling your might as a force in your field. There is a thread that gives you life. You don't even need to understand it, only feel it in the dreams carved into your bones. Taste it in the first strawberries from your garden or the spinach leaves with the tang of minerals from your lettuce patch. See it in the way the robin gathers dry grass for its nest or in the industry of bees sucking down pollen from your fearless hollyhocks; in the way it rains when only sunshine is promised, feeding the earth and allowing your seeds to drink up the evening's sweetness.

Yes to listening to those birds, yes to tuning them out. Yes to the afternoon cup of tea – and yes to a second cup. Yes to losing track of time because your enjoyment makes the circling hands around the clock's face irrelevant. Yes to getting lost in the magic of the day. This is your Yes, that heady tingle of something just beyond your sight that permeates your worldly experience, filling it with light and the warming caress of an afternoon breeze. Here, in the stillness, is your answer. It clears away the dust and doubt, the painfully literal that, like a bookmark, attempts to pin down your story to one set page, when it is an ever-evolving tapestry threading each day with new experience.

So yes to dressing like a fictional character and yes to living out loud. Yes to collecting jewelry and crystals as a magpie collects shiny treasures, and yes to wearing them all at once without rhyme or reason. Yes to writing who knows what – a poem, a list, a story – and enjoying its amorphous exuberance. Yes to living your creed. Yes to the power of your *No* and yes to the power of your *Yes*. It is tempting even to call this Yes transitory, more of that dust and doubt, but it is ever constant in the way it fills you up with breath and possibility. Why not make your Yes the stuff of your everyday? Why not fill your heart with it until there is room for more Yes and more Yes and more Yes?

It is not about the Why, only the Everlasting Yes. The Yes. The Yes. The Yes.

Yes. Just hell yes. You must only feel the Yes.

About the Author

Maria DeBlassie, Ph.D. is a native New Mexican mestiza blogger, writer, and educator living in the Land of Enchantment. Her blogging life started as a year-long journey to write her way back into happy, healthy, and whole through daily posts about life's simple pleasures, everyday magic, and radical self-care. That year-long experiment turned into a lifestyle, a book, a press – and her ongoing blog, Enchantment Learning & Living. She is forever looking for magic in her life and somehow always finding more than she thought was there. Find out more about Maria and conjuring everyday magic at www.mariadeblassie. com

MOON
BOOKS

Moon Books

PAGANISM & SHAMANISM

What is Paganism? A religion, a spirituality, an alternative belief system, nature worship? You can find support for all these definitions (and many more) in dictionaries, encyclopaedias, and text books of religion, but subscribe to any one and the truth will evade you. Above all Paganism is a creative pursuit, an encounter with reality, an exploration of meaning and an expression of the soul. Druids, Heathens, Wiccans and others, all contribute their insights and literary riches to the Pagan tradition. Moon Books invites you to begin or to deepen your own encounter, right here, right now.

If you have enjoyed this book, why not tell other readers by posting a review on your preferred book site. Recent bestsellers from Moon Books are:

Journey to the Dark Goddess
How to Return to Your Soul
Jane Meredith
Discover the powerful secrets of the Dark Goddess and transform your depression, grief and pain into healing and integration.
Paperback: 978-1-84694-677-6 ebook: 978-1-78099-223-5

Shamanic Reiki
Expanded Ways of Working with Universal Life Force Energy
Llyn Roberts, Robert Levy
Shamanism and Reiki are each powerful ways of healing; together,
their power multiplies. Shamanic Reiki introduces techniques to
help healers and Reiki practitioners tap ancient healing wisdom.
Paperback: 978-1-84694-037-8 ebook: 978-1-84694-650-9

Pagan Portals – The Awen Alone
Walking the Path of the Solitary Druid
Joanna van der Hoeven
An introductory guide for the solitary Druid, The Awen Alone
will accompany you as you explore, and seek out your own place
within the natural world.
Paperback: 978-1-78279-547-6 ebook: 978-1-78279-546-9

A Kitchen Witch's World of Magical Herbs & Plants
Rachel Patterson
A journey into the magical world of herbs and plants, filled with
magical uses, folklore, history and practical magic. By popular
writer, blogger and kitchen witch, Tansy Firedragon.
Paperback: 978-1-78279-621-3 ebook: 978-1-78279-620-6

Medicine for the Soul
The Complete Book of Shamanic Healing
Ross Heaven
All you will ever need to know about shamanic healing and how to
become your own shaman…
Paperback: 978-1-78099-419-2 ebook: 978-1-78099-420-8

Shaman Pathways – The Druid Shaman
Exploring the Celtic Otherworld
Danu Forest
A practical guide to Celtic shamanism with exercises and
techniques as well as traditional lore for exploring the Celtic
Otherworld.
Paperback: 978-1-78099-615-8 ebook: 978-1-78099-616-5

Traditional Witchcraft for the Woods and Forests
A Witch's Guide to the Woodland with Guided Meditations and
Pathworking
Melusine Draco
A Witch's guide to walking alone in the woods, with guided
meditations and pathworking.
Paperback: 978-1-84694-803-9 ebook: 978-1-84694-804-6

Wild Earth, Wild Soul
A Manual for an Ecstatic Culture
Bill Pfeiffer
Imagine a nature-based culture so alive and so connected,
spreading like wildfire. This book is the first flame...
Paperback: 978-1-78099-187-0 ebook: 978-1-78099-188-7

Naming the Goddess
Trevor Greenfield
Naming the Goddess is written by over eighty adherents and
scholars of Goddess and Goddess Spirituality.
Paperback: 978-1-78279-476-9 ebook: 978-1-78279-475-2

Shapeshifting into Higher Consciousness
Heal and Transform Yourself and Our World with Ancient
Shamanic and Modern Methods
Llyn Roberts
Ancient and modern methods that you can use every day to trans-
form yourself and make a positive difference in the world.
Paperback: 978-1-84694-843-5 ebook: 978-1-84694-844-2

Readers of ebooks can buy or view any of these bestsellers by
clicking on the live link in the title. Most titles are published in
paperback and as an ebook. Paperbacks are available in traditional
bookshops. Both print and ebook formats are available online.

Find more titles and sign up to our readers' newsletter at
http://www.johnhuntpublishing.com/paganism
Follow us on Facebook at https://www.facebook.com/MoonBooks
and Twitter at https://twitter.com/MoonBooksJHP